CAL

Celebrating the career
of a baseball legend

To all of our heroes.

CAL

Celebrating the career of a baseball legend

Photo credits

T = top, B = bottom, C = center, L = left, R = right.

The Baltimore Sun

Karl Merton Ferron: 3, 16, 17, 19, 20, 22-23, 29, 41T, 41B, 50, 52, 58-59, 73, 78, 80BL, 96, 118-119, 121.

Doug Kapustin: 8-9, 32, 45B, 70, 114.

Lloyd Fox: 10-11, 57L, 77, 81TR, 80CL, 81BL, 97, 101, 117.

Elizabeth Malby: 14, 34, 39, 42, 44, 45T, 47.

J. Pat Carter: 21, 142, 152, 153, 154.

John Makely: 24, 25, 27, 40, 46, 55, 60, 62-63, 65, 68, 71, 72, 85, 86T, 86B, 87, 99, 109.

Gene Sweeney Jr.: 28, 35, 53, 56, 57R, 61B, 79, 80TL, 80C, 82-83, 84, 94, 111T, 115, 126, 138, 145, 149, 150, 155, 166.

Perry E. Thorsvik: 38, 92.

Kenneth K. Lam: 57C, 80BR, 81BR, 90, 100, 116, 122.

Jed Kirschbaum: 64B, 108, 111B, 147.

Michael Lutzky: 80TC, 81CR.

Garo Lachinian: 95.

Amy Davis: 98, 139, 168.

Jeffrey F. Bill: 106.

Robert K. Hamilton: 136, 148.

Irving H. Phillips Jr.: 146.

Paul Hutchins: 160.

Baltimore Sun Staff photo: 18.

The Sporting News

Albert Dickson: 4-5, 26, 36, 37, 43, 158, 161, 162, 163, 164, 165, 167, 169, 170, 171.

Bob Leverone: 76, 120, 174-175.

Dilip Vishwanat: 110.

The Sporting News Archives: 54, 74, 75, 93, 102-103, 112-113, 137.

Baltimore Orioles: 151.

Associated Press
Chris Stanfield: 61T.
Roberto Borea: 64T.

Photos courtesy of Vi Ripken: 128, 129, 130 (all), 131, 132, 133, 134, 135, 144.

Published by The Sporting News, 10176 Corporate Square Drive, Suite 200, St. Louis, MO 63132, and The Baltimore Sun Company, 501 North Calvert Street, Baltimore, MD 21278.

The Sporting News is a federally regisistered trademark of Vulcan Sports Media, Inc. Visit our website at www.sportingnews.com. SunSpot, the online service of The Baltimore Sun, can be found at www.sunspot.net.

ISBN: 0-89204-642-2

Acknowledgements

It seems somehow fitting that it took so many talented people from *The Baltimore Sun* and *The Sporting News* to put this book together about a single extraordinary player. Just like Cal Ripken's teammates and managers came and went along his career, some of the writers and photographers and editors who chronicled his baseball life came and went as well. To chronicle that baseball life, we—*The Sun* and *The Sporting News*—assembled an All-Star cast, an All-Star cast that experienced not only the drama and excitement of Cal's most shining moments, but a cast whose members were there when no one else was. There can be no better crew assembled than this:

• Ken Rosenthal is a senior writer who covers national baseball for *The Sporting News.* Before TSN, Ken was a columnist for nine years at *The Sun* and covered the Orioles for the paper for four years. Ken's regional and national perspective on Cal's career gives him a unique viewpoint from which to write The Legend and The Icon chapters of this book.

• Joe Strauss, who wrote The End and The Offense chapters, has been *The Sun's* Orioles beat writer since 1997. He has covered all of the significant moments in Cal's career in the past five years, including his move from shortstop to third base, the end of his consecutive-games streak, his 6-for-6 game, his 400th homer and his 3,000th hit.

• Peter Schmuck, who wrote The Streak and The Defense, has been covering major league baseball since 1979 for *The Sun* and the *Orange County* (Calif.) *Register.* He was the Orioles beat writer for *The Sun* from 1990 to 1993 and has been its national baseball reporter since 1994. He covered Cal's 2,131st consecutive game and the games in which he collected his 400th home run and 3,000th hit. Peter also reported on Cal's only World Series appearance in 1983 and was present for 18 of Ripken's 19 All-Star Games.

• Michael Knisley, senior writer for *The Sporting News,* covered Cal for the magazine during his chase for the consecutive-games record. He brings that national perspective to Ripken in the chapter The Stage.

• Mike Klingaman, a news and sports reporter for *The Evening Sun* and *Sun* for 30 years, first wrote about Cal in the 1970s, when Cal was in high school. During the course of reporting several stories on Cal, Mike has spoken numerous times with every member of Cal's immediate family, and with that background, he contributes the chapter The Family.

• John Eisenberg, who wrote The Young Wonder chapter, has been covering sports in Baltimore since 1984 and been a sports columnist for *The Sun* since 1987. He has covered Cal throughout his record-setting streak and has reported on Ripken at numerous All-Star Games and in the postseason.

These guys were the nucleus of our team, but like every true successful team, we had many others who contributed along the way. Without their work and desire, this project would never have happened.

From *The Sun,* Jim Preston and Jerry Jackson spent countless hours editing thousands of images from *The Sun's* photographers who have shot Orioles games and Cal's career from Day One. Ray Frager's editing and organizing brought this project together. Debbie Golumbek and Cari Pierce kept the project afloat during the uncertain period of Cal's final seasons. And, finally, there is Molly Dunham, who helped initiate this project so long ago that Cal's streak was still in place at the time.

From *The Sporting News,* Bob Parajon provided the art direction for the book, and designer Christen Sager carried it through from cover to cover. Joe Hoppel edited, organized and put a lot of detail work into it. TSN photographers Albert Dickson, Robert Seale, Dilip Vishwanat and Bob Leverone's photographs capture Cal not just on the field but off the field as well, and prepress specialist Dave Brickey made sure those images reproduced brilliantly on each page, with an assist from Steve Romer.

Together, this team captures Cal's extraordinary baseball career like no other before it.

Contents

Foreword

By Brooks Robinson

Maybe the greatest thing about following Cal Ripken Jr. from the beginning of his major league career has been watching him grow. He has gone from a Rookie of the Year to a two-time MVP to a record-breaker and, now, with his career over, to a place among the greats of baseball.

I first met Cal when he was a teenager, when he came to the ballpark with his dad, Cal Sr., one of our Orioles coaches. I talked to his father about him and followed his career in the minors. Later, as an Orioles television announcer, I saw Cal break into the big leagues and watched him regularly.

Cal is baseball through and through, one of the many wonderful traits he inherited from his dad. He was always determined to play the game the right way. And he had that stubborn streak, which led to his famous consecutive-games streak. The way Cal figured, if there's a game, you want to play.

His streak of 2,632 games, well, I can't fathom that at all. That's about eight times as many games as I ever played in a row.

For all of Cal's talent, he never took anything for granted, never assumed anything. He just kept working at it. Look at the way he'd alter his batting stances over his career. That's an example of a guy constantly working on his game—if one thing doesn't work, you try something else.

And consider how he played defense. It was overshadowed some by his hitting and the way people focused on his being such a big man playing a little man's position at shortstop. But I played with some great shortstops—Luis Aparicio, Mark Belanger—and I think Cal's right there with them.

He was smart, had great hands and then there was that instinct you've almost got to be born with—he was where the ball was.

Cal did all this—the hitting, the fielding, The Streak—under much more pressure than we had in my day. Players have so many more demands, yet it never seemed to show on Cal.

It was fitting he was the one to break Lou Gehrig's record. I always respected Gehrig more than any other player, and Cal just kind of followed in Gehrig's footsteps.

Cal will go down as one of the all-time greats of the game, and it has been a pleasure to watch him. I've heard he has said I was a role model for him. That is an honor, because he's a role model for all of baseball.

Brooks Robinson

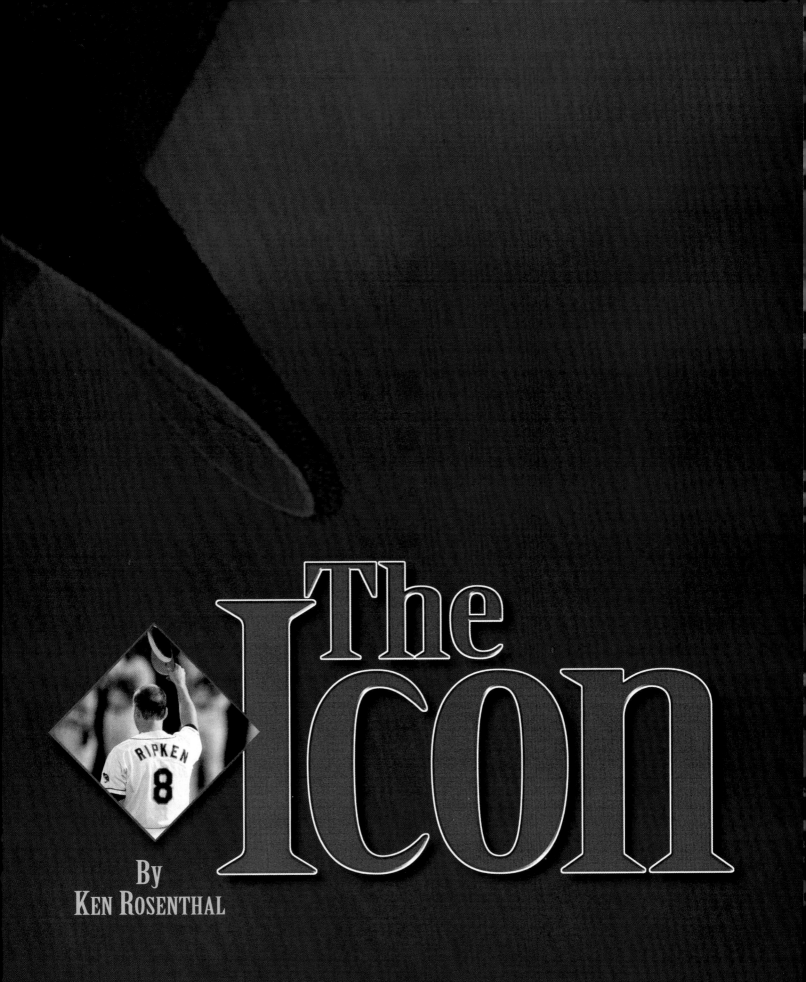

The Icon

By
Ken Rosenthal

1

The Icon

He played in a video-highlight age, but no single replay could capture his greatness. Mammoth home runs defined Mark McGwire. Acrobatic defensive plays defined Ozzie Smith. Cal Ripken was capable of such feats—and many others—on a baseball field. But his 21-year career is best viewed as a long, satisfying movie, as opposed to a 10-second clip. What made Ripken great was his consistency. His dependability. His determination to help his team win, each and every day.

Like any baseball player, Ripken will be remembered for his numbers—3,184 hits, 431 home runs and, most of all, 2,632 consecutive games. But Ripken never was a conventional player, and he can't be measured by conventional standards. His statistics were Hall of Fame caliber, but his contributions to his team, city and sport put him in a category beyond. Ripken embodied practically all of the virtues that fans desire in star athletes—diligence and intelligence, loyalty and humility. Virtues that too often are the exception in professional sports. Virtues that elevated him to the loftiest ideal, America's vision of what a baseball player should be.

His name was written into the Orioles' lineup as if etched in granite. His managers and teammates drew strength from his presence the way children draw comfort from their parents. Ripken refused to take a day off even against top pitchers like Nolan Ryan and Randy Johnson. He spent countless hours in the batting cage before games and in the weight room afterward. Until the very end of his career, he was seemingly invulnerable to injury. And if the opposition had the bases loaded with two outs in the bottom of the ninth inning, the Orioles wanted the ball hit to him, and nowhere else.

During periods of reflection, Cal Ripken could look back on his consistency, dependability and determination.

Fans appreciated Ripken's skill, his ability to hit for average and power at a position where defense had always taken priority; his thinking man's approach to shortstop, where he used superior positioning to cover every angle. But more than anything else, they appreciated his sensibility, how he always seemed to put family first and never forgot what it was like to cheer for his hometown Orioles as a boy attending games at Baltimore's old Memorial Stadium.

The Streak (opposite page) was Ripken's defining achievement, but he won fans over in many other ways, too—including his willingness to sign countless autographs.

Ripken signed countless autographs in an era when players routinely charged for their signatures. He spent his entire career with the Orioles in an era when future Hall of Famers frequently changed teams. He never complained about his contract, never criticized others for their shortcomings. And he gave his sport a rallying point when it needed one most, in the aftermath of a players strike in 1994 and '95.

The Streak, of course, was Ripken's defining achievement, climaxing with what Roger Clemens called "our generation's great moment"—September 6, 1995, the night Ripken broke Lou Gehrig's consecutive-games record at Camden Yards. Baseball was at its best that night, linking the present to the past, elevating a player to mythic status, offering an object lesson to the nation.

Ripken, too, was at his best, handling the moment with exquisite grace. The game was nationally televised, and the images remain indelible. Ripken removing his white Orioles jersey to reveal a T-shirt that said, "2,130+, Hugs and Kisses for Daddy." Teammates Rafael Palmeiro and Bobby Bonilla pushing him out of the dugout for a victory lap around the ballpark. Ripken's father, Cal Ripken Sr., clapping and waving from his luxury box, biting his lower lip to fight back tears.

Simon and Garfunkel once sang, "Where have you gone, Joe DiMaggio? A nation turns its lonely eyes to you." Ripken filled the void left by DiMaggio that night, with the great Yankee Clipper—a former teammate of Gehrig's—in attendance. Grown men had cried at Gehrig's retirement ceremony 56 years before, but those tears were born out of tragedy, the knowledge that Gehrig was seriously ill. The tears of September 6, 1995, were born out of joy and love and

The Icon

hometown pride.

And yet, it was only one night. One night in a streak that began on May 30, 1982, before the rise of all-sports radio, all-sports television and the Internet. One game in a career that began during Ronald Reagan's first term and ended during George W. Bush's first term. One scene from a movie in which the leading man never required an understudy, combining the physical strength of Arnold Schwarzenegger with the mental toughness of John Wayne.

The movie about Gehrig was called "The Pride of the Yankees." For a movie about Ripken, such a title would be too confining. He wasn't just the pride of the Orioles. He became the pride of his city, the pride of his state, the pride of baseball.

◆ ◆ ◆

How did it all begin? How did one man develop the attributes not only to play 2,632 consecutive games, but also to start every one? The answers lay with Ripken's father, the crusty,

The strength and resolve of Cal Ripken Sr. were great influences on his son, who learned that doing things the right way— The Oriole Way— involved more than a perfect attendance record.

indefatigable Cal Ripken Sr., who died in March 1999 at age 63.

The elder Ripken spent more than half of his life in the Orioles' organization, and he became one of the great instructors the game has ever known. His guiding philosophy was a system of fundamentals called "The Oriole Way," which became the foundation of the franchise's glory years from 1966 through '83. The team attempted to restore its tradition when it hired Ripken Sr. as manager in '87 (and subsequent managers with strong ties to the past). Most of its attempts failed, but one vestige of "The Oriole Way" remained through the '90s—Cal Jr., the oldest of Senior's three sons.

Junior went the equivalent of more than 16 seasons without a day off, but it was no accident that his work ethic involved more than a perfect attendance record. His father didn't settle for the old bromide "practice makes perfect." He preached "perfect practice makes perfect." And though he stood only 5-11 and weighed 170 pounds–-five inches shorter and 50 pounds lighter than Cal Jr.—his strength and resolve were legendary in the Baltimore organization.

As a minor leaguer, Ripken Sr. once volunteered to catch three straight doubleheaders—six games in three days. Nearly three decades later, during his brief tenure as Orioles manager, he was asked what would happen if he were trapped in a

The Icon

room with a Doberman. The dog, Senior said, "wouldn't have a chance."

On a winter day when Cal Jr. was 16, Senior went out to plow snow, and the crank on the tractor broke off as he was turning it, smashing into his forehead and opening a bloody wound. Junior pleaded with his father to go to the hospital, but Senior would have nothing of it. He applied an oily rag to the wound, walked to the house to get some bandages, then returned to finish plowing.

Imagine, then, growing up as one of his four children, 30 miles northeast of Baltimore in Aberdeen, Md.—Ellen was the oldest, followed by Cal Jr., Fred and Bill. In his rare moments away from the ballpark, Senior would gather the boys in the back yard and hit them grounder after grounder, ignoring any complaints if minor injuries occurred. "The ball weighs only 5¼ ounces," Senior would say. "How much can it hurt?"

Senior wasn't the only powerful welder who forged the Iron Man. Ripken's mother, Vi, raised four children alone for months at a time, then packed them into the family's old Mercury every summer to join Senior wherever he was stationed as a minor league player or manager. Yet, who can explain why Cal Jr. became a 19-time All-Star selection and Fred a motorcycle mechanic? Why Cal Jr. almost never got hurt, while Bill was frequently injured during his own 12-year major league career?

For all the qualities that Junior inherited from Senior—and the powerful physique that set him apart from his father and brothers—he also benefited from

Cal Sr. and Vi combined to forge the Iron Man, passing along qualities that served him well as a major leaguer. It wasn't all good genes and hard work, though. Cal Jr. also benefited from some luck along the way.

a certain amount of luck, dating to the formative stages of his career.

When he was a senior at Aberdeen High School, most major league scouts projected Ripken as a pitcher. The late Dick Bowie, a scout for the Orioles, held the minority opinion—that the gangly 17-year-old should be tried as a shortstop and switched back to a pitcher only if he failed to establish himself as an everyday player.

Forty-seven players were selected ahead of Ripken in the 1978 amateur draft, including three by the Orioles. The debate over Ripken's position continued as he ascended through the minor leagues, playing mostly shortstop initially, then mostly third base at the higher levels. The Orioles envisioned a future infield featuring Ripken at third and Bob Bonner at short. But in the summer of 1982, Baltimore manager Earl Weaver made a change no one else in the organization favored, installing Ripken at shortstop. It was a decision that Ripken would justify every day for the next 14 seasons, a decision that changed major league history. Ripken played so well from the start that he was voted the 1982 American League Rookie of the Year.

Years later, he would recall that he might not have gotten the chance to play shortstop with another team and that he might have injured his arm as a pitcher and never reached the majors.

At 6-4, Ripken was touted as the tallest player ever to play shortstop regularly in the majors. But then, who could have imagined him elsewhere? The son of Cal Ripken Sr. was meant to play one of the most active positions on the field. He wasn't meant to be a pitcher, taking a baseball into his hands only every fifth day.

◆ ◆ ◆

From the start, Ripken stood tall—unusually tall—at shortstop. By his second full season in the majors, he was playing in the World Series against the Phillies and Joe Morgan.

The first line on Ripken's Hall of Fame plaque will describe him as the player who broke Gehrig's consecutive-games record. The casual fan will remember him in much the same way, failing to grasp the underlying reality of The Streak—that it became possible only because Ripken was a great player and that he

would have become a Hall of Famer even without it.

Some argued that Ripken's offensive statistics might have been even better if he had taken an occasional day off. Others pointed out that The Streak gave him the extra at-bats necessary to reach 400 homers and 3,000 hits. Such contradictions were typical of Ripken's career. He left his mark on the game by bringing power to a traditionally light-hitting position. And yet, defense was always his forte.

Ripken finished his career with one major league hitting record—345 home runs by a shortstop—but he boasted 11 major league or American League fielding records. He never won a batting title, a home run title or an RBI title. But in 1990, he produced probably the best defensive season by a shortstop in major league history, committing only three errors in 680 chances. Ripken's idol, Orioles Hall of Fame third baseman Brooks Robinson, once made three errors in a game.

Some thought Ripken too big and too slow to play an adequate shortstop, and he was always underappreciated as a defender, winning only two Gold Gloves. But he had all the essential tools—soft hands, keen reactions, a powerful arm. He wasn't as quick as Ozzie Smith, the other preeminent shortstop of the '80s, who was 70 pounds lighter. For Ripken to succeed at short, he almost had to redefine the way the position was played, create a scientific ballet that enabled him to make the difficult look routine. He did just that, shifting his position on each

The Icon

pitch, recalibrating his angle according to the pitcher, the hitter, the count and the game situation.

The result was one "6-3" on the scorecard after another, a monotony that kept Ripken off the 11 o'clock highlights but helped the Orioles win games. If he lacked range, it almost never showed. Ripken's positioning was so superior, he rarely needed to make spectacular stops, hardly ever dived for ground balls. Yet, his defense was utterly compelling, and Ripken developed his own trademarks. His pinpoint-accurate throws from deep in the shortstop hole. His 360-degree spins that returned him to proper throwing position on grounders hit up the middle. His soccer-style slides toward balls that fell in the outfield, again enabling him to come up throwing. No one was better at retreating for popups, even when it meant venturing into foul territory.

Ripken worked at his defense, never missing infield practice, but his fielding came more naturally than his hitting. It wasn't that Ripken lacked ability at the plate. He had all the requisite tools; strong hands, good hand-eye coordination, sharp concentration. It's just that he wasn't as gifted as Wade Boggs or Tony Gwynn, the two leading average hitters of his day.

Ripken's .276 career batting average is the lowest of any member of the 3,000-hit club. His swing was more effort than elegance, and he constantly tinkered with his stance and mechanics, enduring some horrific slumps. But he

Ripken finished his career with one major league hitting record—345 home runs by a shortstop—but he boasted 11 major league or American League fielding records.

also produced more than his share of stirring, transcendent moments at the plate.

Consider his first decade: Ripken led the A.L. in hits, doubles and runs in 1983 and captured his first Most Valuable Player award as the Orioles won the World Series. He hit a three-run homer off Roger Clemens on opening day to trigger the Orioles' surprising 1989 season, when they finished second after losing 107 games the previous year. And he put together his second MVP season

A tinkerer at the plate and a man who endured some sizable slumps, Ripken had the knack of coming up big offensively in dramatic situations.

in 1991, a year in which he also was named MVP in the All-Star Game after hitting a three-run homer to lead the American League to a 4-2 victory.

Now consider his second decade: Ripken hit home runs on both the night he tied Gehrig's record and the night he broke it. He batted .348 in the 1997 American League Championship Series just months after he nearly ended The Streak because of lower back pain. He went a career-best 6-for-6 in Atlanta in June 1999. In the Orioles-Braves game that night, ESPN used a computer to measure players' bat speed, how quickly they moved the bat through the strike zone. Ripken, then 38, and the Braves' Andruw Jones, then 22, were the fastest. Three months later, Ripken underwent major back surgery. Despite being hobbled throughout '99, he wound up batting a remarkable .340 in 86 games. And then there was the 2001 All-Star Game, in which the retirement-bound Ripken again showed his flair for the dramatic—indeed, the spine-tingling—by homering on the first pitch he saw on the way to winning MVP honors. Just three weeks earlier, Ripken had announced he would retire at year's end, meaning this would be his 19th and last time in uniform as a member of the A.L. All-Stars. He made it a memorable night.

◆ ◆ ◆

Ask former teammates what it was like to play with the Iron Man, and one of the first things they'll mention is Ripken's legendary competitiveness.

As a child, Ripken displayed a killer instinct playing cards, jacks or Monopoly. In his first year of minor league baseball, he went bowling with a teammate and rigged the scoring computer to give himself a perfect 300 game.

Once he became a star, Ripken built a house that included a full-court gymnasium, and he held five-on-five games in which the participants wore official NBA jerseys.

The Icon

Ripken's competitive streak obviously served him well in his countdown to Gehrig, but it was perhaps even more of an asset in enabling him to overcome his sporadic batting funks. Not that Ripken was immune from lapses in confidence. He thought his days as a player might be nearing an end when he was batting .209 in June 1990. And he was so embarrassed to be batting .215 a week before the 1993 All-Star Game that he said he would have considered withdrawing if the game had not been in Baltimore.

But just when it appeared that Ripken might need a day off—or might be declining as a player—he would rise out of his crouch and swat away any criticism and doubt.

Toward the end of his career, Ripken faced a new and uncomfortable challenge—back problems that forced him to confront his baseball mortality. He made his first two trips to the disabled list in '99 and underwent surgery on September 23 of that season. But partly through his work with hitting coach Terry Crowley, Ripken sustained, and even expanded, his hitting prowess (along with his lofty batting average, he had a .584 slugging percentage). And he accomplished this at age 39. Few other players used their wills to enhance their skills in such fashion.

Was Ripken a great hitter? Maybe not in the classic sense. But only six other

Ask former teammates about Ripken, and one of the first things they will mention is his competitiveness. Cal played full-bore, as Cleveland's Omar Vizquel (or anyone else trying to complete a double play) found out.

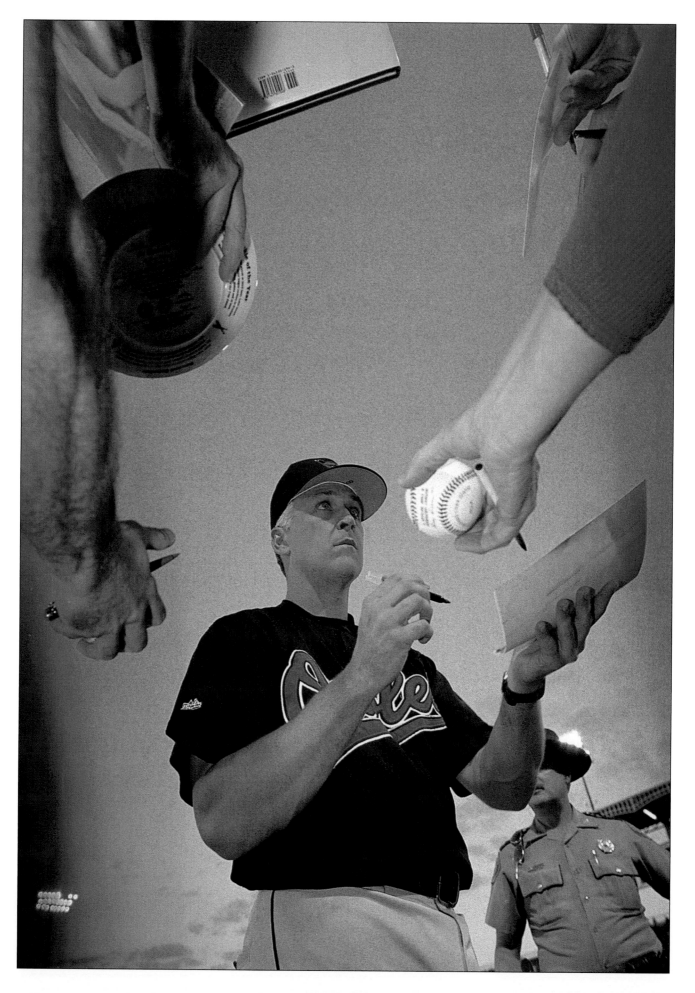

major leaguers reached the 3,000-hit/400-homer plateau: Hank Aaron, Willie Mays, Eddie Murray, Stan Musial, Dave Winfield and Carl Yastrzemski. None was a middle infielder for the majority of his career. None redefined his position like Ripken.

◆ ◆ ◆

The scene was common in summer '95: Ripken remaining in his uniform after a game, then returning to the field and signing autographs into the night.

The autograph sessions took place at home and on the road. They weren't scheduled, and they weren't publicized. They just happened, serving as an olive branch to fans still angry with major league baseball for the players strike in 1994 and '95. And they came at a point when the demands on Ripken's time had never been greater, as his countdown to Gehrig neared its conclusion.

"Late Night With Cal" was a sight to behold, especially at Camden Yards, where fans would form lines more than 100 yards long, up the aisle and into the concourse, with kids playing catch as they waited for Ripken's autograph.

Three years later, Mark McGwire and Sammy Sosa displayed uncommon sportsmanship during their record-breaking home run race, and they were credited with reviving baseball. But McGwire and Sosa were only completing the job that Ripken started in '95, a job he took as seriously and performed as successfully as his actual baseball duties.

To hear Ripken tell it, he no more saw himself as baseball's savior than he did as Gehrig's conqueror; he reached those pinnacles by relying on his core values,

"Late Night With Cal" and other such fan-friendly sessions showed that Ripken always seemed to do the right thing—which, considering the public's anger over the 1994 strike, proved to be an immense public relations boost for baseball.

his belief that players had a responsibility to their fans, his desire to help the Orioles every day. In an age when superstar athletes frequently engaged in self-centered behavior and even criminal misconduct, Ripken always seemed to do the right thing. Fans couldn't help but notice, and after Ripken broke Gehrig's record, he was routinely cheered as a visiting player, even in normally hostile parks like Yankee Stadium. But naturally, he was most beloved in Baltimore,

Ripken made friends (feathered and otherwise) at home and on the road. He was routinely cheered as a visiting player, even in normally hostile parks like Yankee Stadium.

a city that lacked an NFL franchise for much of his career. A city that lost its baseball glory after the Orioles won that '83 Series crown. A city that viewed Ripken as the embodiment of its blue-collar ethic. A city Ripken that was proud to call home.

Almost all of the great players of his era—McGwire, Barry Bonds, Ken Griffey Jr, Greg Maddux, Randy Johnson and Pedro Martinez—changed teams at one time or another, most because of contract differences. In a sense, Ripken was fortunate; the Orioles could always afford his salary as they evolved into a large-market team with the opening of Camden Yards in 1992. Still, he was determined to spend his entire career with one club, like Brooks Robinson did. Ripken re-signed with the Orioles three months after they fired his father as manager in '88. He re-signed after prolonged and distracting contract negotiations during the '92 season. He played in only one World Series, then spent his final 18 seasons trying to return to baseball's showcase event. But he never bailed on the team.

Just as Ripken wasn't immune from disappointment—he figured he would play in the Series every year after winning it in his second full season—he wasn't immune from controversy. The Streak was a paradox that combined elements of

The Icon

selfishness and selflessness. Calls for Ripken to end his quest would surface whenever he stopped hitting or appeared hurt. And other, peripheral issues occasionally arose. Ripken's unique status helped create a double standard that divided the clubhouse after the Orioles acquired other prominent stars in the mid-'90s. He hardly spoke with Manny Alexander, a shortstop who threatened to replace him. He initially resisted moving to third base.

Through it all, Ripken escaped with his image untarnished—the issues that surrounded him never were significant enough for anyone to stop viewing him as a symbol of all that was good about the game.

The Streak grew so big, though, that it seemed no one knew how to end it. But Ripken found a way on September 20, 1998, bringing his achievement to a proper and graceful conclusion by sitting out the Orioles' final home game. He seemed even more mortal the next season, when he grieved the loss of his father and confronted his first major injury. Yet he hit his 400th homer in September 1999, and he delivered his 3,000th hit in April 2000. Each milestone turned into a celebration of Ripken, the credits rolling at the close of an epic career.

The movie is over now. Cal Ripken Jr. is retired. But like all classics, his legacy should prove everlasting. Ripken paved the way for Alex Rodriguez, Derek Jeter and other tall shortstops by proving that a big man could play the position. And he set a record for the ages, a record that came to define him. No one will ever play that many consecutive games again.

No one will even try.

Gehrig's monument at Yankee Stadium says his "amazing record of 2,130 consecutive games should stand for all time." Ripken reduced forever to 56 years, and he turned his 16½ years of never missing a game into a new forever.

Cal Ripken's consistency was his majesty. His greatness extended beyond mere baseball skill. He was there for his team, there for his city, there for his sport. Each and every day.

Gehrig's monument at Yankee Stadium says his "amazing record of 2,130 consecutive games should stand for all time." Ripken reduced forever to 56 years, and he turned his 16½ years of never missing a game into a new forever.

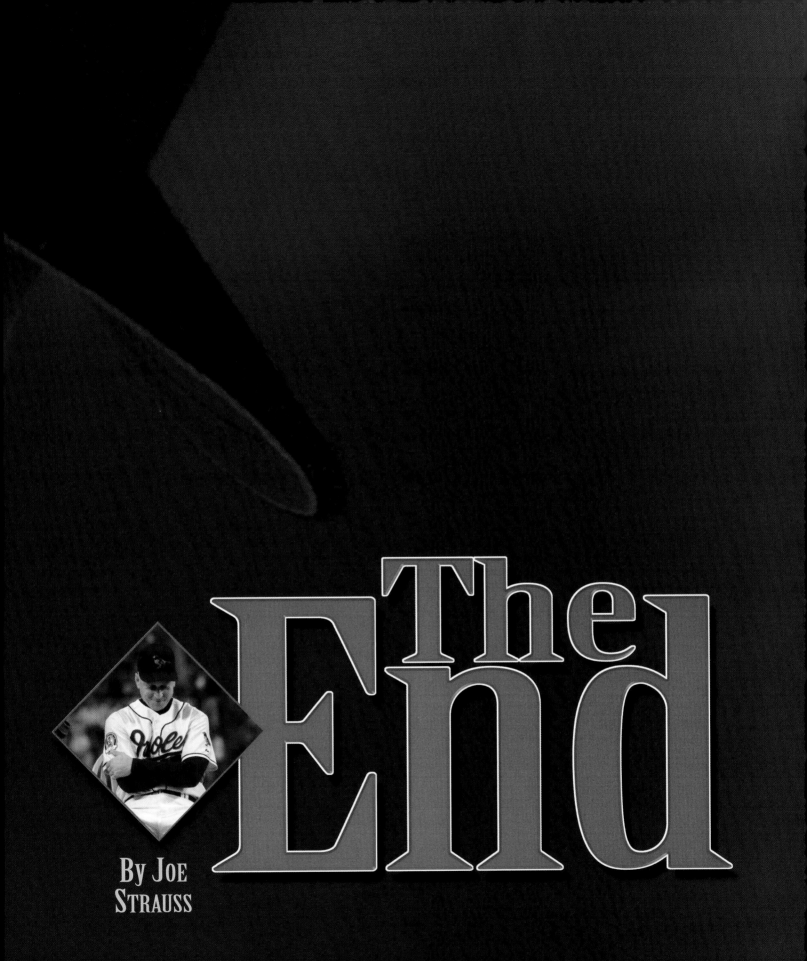

The End

By Joe
Strauss

The End

And so it drew to a close.

No more "big, round numbers" to chase, no more seasons to anticipate. Only an indelible moment to enjoy 7,363 days after his major league career began.

One more time, the reception he had come to know and many of the faces he had come to recognize during the past 21 seasons touched Cal Ripken at Camden Yards. Many of the younger ones were there to celebrate the end of Ripken's Hall of Fame career, while many of their elders saw it not only as the completion of a playing life, but also of a lineage. Moments after the Orioles concluded an otherwise faceless 2001 season with a 5-1 loss to the Boston Red Sox on October 6, Ripken stood behind a podium placed between shortstop and third base to tender his goodbye.

"Tonight we close a chapter of this dream—my playing career. But I have other dreams," said Ripken, 41 years old and balding but still fit and energized by the game. "I might have some white hair on top of this head; well, maybe on the sides of the head. But I'm not really that old. My dreams for the future include me pursuing my passion for baseball (initially, anyway, through a youth baseball complex). Hopefully, I will be able to share what I have learned, and I would be happy if that sharing would lead to something as simple as a smile on the face of others."

Baltimore has always embraced each of its baseball stars as one of its own. But Ripken's status was natural. He *is* one of the city's own.

Even before he became the legacy to a tradition begun by Brooks Robinson, Jim Palmer and Eddie Murray, Ripken had Orioles baseball in his blood thanks to the influence of his father, Cal Sr., a man

Cal Ripken Jr.'s long goodbye as an active player included some unexpected—and shocking—twists.

When the tributes and a storied career came to an end on October 6, Ripken appeared particularly contemplative.

The End

During Ripken's news conference on June 19 to confirm his decision to retire at season's end, he and his wife Kelly enjoyed a light exchange with the media.

who embodied the fundamental, uncompromising approach to the game known as The Oriole Way. Now, 4½ decades after Cal Sr. began the family's bond with the franchise, the son stood before a darkened crowd as a civic treasure and national icon.

It had taken Ripken 21 seasons to amass 3,184 hits, 431 home runs and 1,695 RBIs and 16 years to achieve the 2,632 consecutive-game streak that came to define him. Thinking of that and much more, he gathered himself four times before beginning his speech. He ended his brief remarks poignantly and simply, concluding: "One question I've repeatedly been asked these last few weeks is how do I want to be remembered. My answer has been simple: To be remembered at all is pretty special. I might also add that if I am remembered, I hope it's because by living my dream I was able to make a difference. Thank you."

And he was gone.

The long goodbye ended nearly four months after Ripken made official his decision to end his two-decade-plus career. Much had happened to his city, his franchise and his country—so much, in fact, that his farewell appearance came in front of a weepy Camden Yards crowd. Three July home games were postponed by a chemical fire from an underground train derailment only several hundred

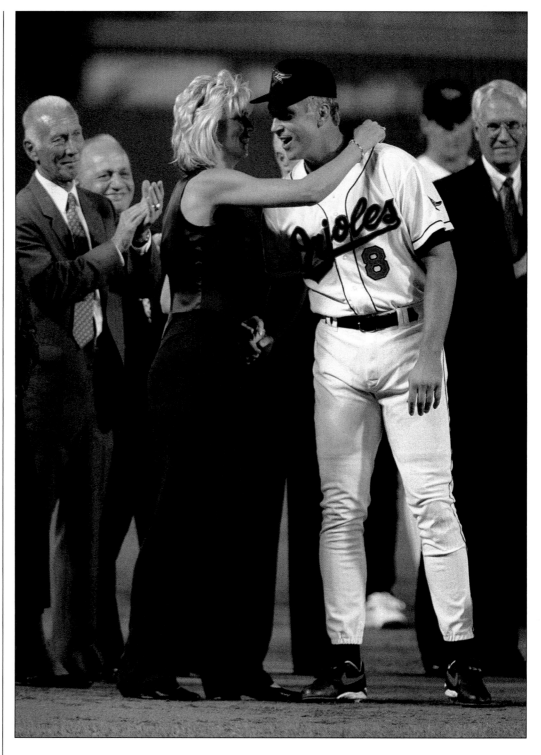

Ripken always tried to keep his family close at hand—as was evident at ceremonies and events celebrating his consecutive-games record—but baseball's brutal travel schedule made it difficult at times. After 21 major league seasons, enough was enough.

The End

yards from the park. After overachieving during a 40-47 first half, a rebuilding Orioles team collapsed after the All-Star break and suffered its fourth consecutive losing season. Baltimore's record, which declined each of those years, plummeted to 63-98 in 2001.

Ripken's final game had been scheduled for September 30 at Yankee Stadium until the September 11 terrorist attacks on the World Trade Center and the Pentagon (40 miles southwest of Camden Yards) caused Major League Baseball to postpone six days' worth of games until the first week of October.

None of the events could have been imagined as Ripken sat beside his wife,

Kelly, at a June 19 news conference to confirm his decision while reflecting on his reasoning.

"I didn't want to be in a position at the end of my career and regret going about it in a certain way," he said. "When I look back over my career, I tried to maximize my playing opportunity and tried to love every moment I had on the field. So when I look back, I don't have those kinds of regrets. I accomplished what my skills, my ability and my determination allowed me to, and I'm proud of the experience."

Ripken arrived at his decision by sensing a pull rather than a push. His wife and two children, Rachel and Ryan, had shared him with the game's brutal travel schedule long enough.

Cal and Kelly discussed his decision for weeks before his public announcement. When Ripken asked his son for input, the little lefthander asked, "What if the Orioles need you?"

Ripken thought of Cal Sr. whenever he put on his uniform. Dad was Cal Jr.'s former coach and manager (and even his protector, when umpires threatened to eject him).

The End

Before he could ponder Ryan's question, Ripken's ego was knocked down a flight of steps by his son's follow-up. "What happens if (first baseman David) Segui gets hurt and they've got to move (Jeff) Conine to first and you've got to play third?"

"I think they'll find somebody else," Ripken said.

Having learned of Ripken's retirement plan from a Baltimore *Sun* reporter the night before, majority owner Peter Angelos offered the feelings of many through a prepared statement read by club chief operating officer Joe Foss: "The Orioles are proud that he has been an integral, essential part of our team for more than two decades. He will always be a special legacy for the Orioles and our fans. Cal Ripken has shown he loves the game of baseball, but I speak for many when I say

the game of baseball loves him as well."

The announcement—coincidentally delivered on Lou Gehrig's birthday—turned the hourglass upside down on a family's tie to the organization. The Orioles had benefited for 45 years from an association with Cal Ripken Sr. and his sons, Cal Jr. and Bill. Cal Sr., who like his baseball-playing sons graduated from Aberdeen High School, signed with the Orioles in 1956 and began playing in their farm system the next year. The Orioles were still new to Baltimore, having moved there from St. Louis before the 1954 season after 52 years as the Browns. By signing Cal Sr. as a minor league catcher, the Orioles unknowingly had shaken hands with a family whose fingerprints would leave an indelible impression on the franchise.

Rip Sr. never played in the major leagues, but he helped hundreds of others do so by influencing them as instructor, coach and manager. His stern example taught two sons and two generations of players a dogged and exemplary way of playing the game.

Ripken always described himself as "a hometown guy," a description he again used during his retirement announcement. "I can't tell you when the Orioles weren't really, really important to me, because I can't remember that far back," he said. "As far back as my memory allows, the Orioles were it."

More than two years after his death in 1999, the father was never far from the son's thoughts. "I think of him every time I put the uniform on," Ripken said in

Ryan Ripken, who attended an All-Star Game news conference with his famous father, had wondered earlier in the season if retirement was the right thing. After all, the boy figured, a situation just might arise in which the Orioles really needed Cal Ripken in the lineup.

Cal kept signing autographs for appreciative fans until the very end.

August of his last season. The most poignant moment of the night of September 6, 1995—the evening Ripken broke Gehrig's consecutive-games record— occurred when he found his mother and father applauding from their suite at Camden Yards. Seeing his father's unfettered joy and pride so moved the son that he bit both lips to contain his emotion.

Ripken maintained he did not announce his decision in midseason to initiate a farewell tour. Instead, Ripken said he merely wanted to relieve himself of a secret.

On the day he announced his intention to retire at season's end, Ripken was hitting .210 with four home runs. His swing, never mistaken for art, had become long and lacked power. A tendency to "cheat," or start his swing early in order to compensate for a slowed bat, became more pronounced.

The Orioles refused to admit so publicly, but Ripken's struggles hastened their willingness to begin his transition to a part-time player. Manager Mike Hargrove notified Ripken of his thinking on April 22, with the 40-year-old hitting .154 with six RBIs and without a multi-hit game in 15 starts. Vice president of baseball operations Syd Thrift said on May 13 that finding Ripken's successor had "absolutely" become a priority.

The Orioles first tried Mike Kinkade at the position and later claimed third baseman Tony Batista off waivers from the Toronto Blue Jays, but Ripken insisted he only needed at-bats to overcome the effects of a spring training

The End

abbreviated by a rib fracture suffered in a February pickup basketball game.

"I need at-bats on the field to get going," Ripken said. "Very rarely do you find it just in the batting cage."

Ripken found it shortly after unburdening himself of his plans. Hitting coach Terry Crowley and Ripken continued to work extensively on mending his approach.

As happened regularly throughout his career, Ripken raised his performance to a level befitting the moment. On the first stop of his farewell tour, Ripken accepted a seat and a vial of infield dirt from old Comiskey Park. After nearly forgetting the wooden seat after the July 1 ceremony, Ripken contributed his first three-hit game of the season and scored three times in an 11-3 win.

Ripken, who had described his combined .300 average of the previous two seasons as being accompanied by a kind of "magic," began to experience that magic again, game by game, city by city.

The crescendo occurred at the All-Star Game July 10 at Seattle's Safeco

After unburdening himself with the announcement of his forthcoming retirement, Ripken came alive at the plate. The day after meeting with the media, he began a 15-game hitting streak. Later, he hit safely in 16 consecutive games.

Field, with Ripken and San Diego Padres outfielder Tony Gwynn as the centerpiece of emotional festivities. Ripken arrived for his 18th All-Star appearance—he was selected 19 times overall but missed one game because of injury—with the least conspicuous production of any participant. He left it as the game's Most Valuable Player, having authored its most powerful moment.

Appreciating his last step onto the game's national stage, Ripken wanted to be the first player to arrive in the American League clubhouse before the game in order to savor every second. "I've never had the experience of seeing a locker room for this event wake up," Ripken said. "You start to see it come alive. It has a lot of energy, and eventually becomes mass hysteria. That was kind of cool. There's a certain excitement you're looking forward to."

A surprise first inning spent at shortstop—thanks to Alex Rodriguez's prompting—was followed by the night's most stirring

Taking the national stage one last time in the 2001 All-Star Game, Ripken received congratulations after providing the game's signature moment with a third-inning homer.

scene when Ripken faced Los Angeles Dodgers pitcher Chan Ho Park in the third inning of a scoreless game. Park's first-pitch fastball tailed in on Ripken, but not far enough in. With a flash of his hands, accompanied by flashes of thousands of cameras, Ripken lined the pitch into the National League bullpen. The American League would win, 4-1, but Ripken's swing became the night's signature moment.

The game served as a springboard for Ripken. In the Orioles' first series of the second half, he rewarded an enthusiastic Atlanta crowd with two home runs as he bid farewell to Turner Field. In a moment no one could remember happening before, Ripken received two curtain calls from an opponent's fans.

"Unbelievable," Ripken said. "Almost to the point where you feel like you're doing something wrong in the middle of the game."

The End

Ripken homered in five of his first six "farewell" cities. He constructed a 16-game hitting streak, his longest since 1992 and the longest by a 40-something player since Paul Molitor's 17-game run in 1998. Three weeks into August, his average had climbed just shy of his career figure entering the season (.277). At every stop, he was presented contributions to the Cal Ripken Sr. Foundation and gifts of appreciation ranging from Dungeness crabs to a pair of handmade cowboy boots to a series of photographs of his father. The pictures presented him by Florida Marlins general manager Dave Dombrowski proved particularly moving. Seeing his father pictured in 1967 as manager of the Orioles' former Class A affiliate, the Miami Marlins, Ripken observed, "I guess I really do look like my dad."

Even within the Orioles' miserable second half,

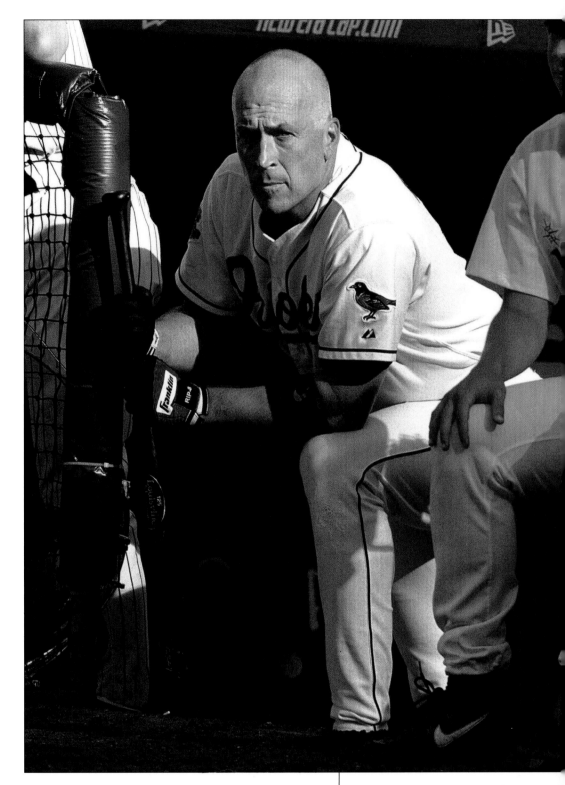

Ripken could not ignore the pull of each ballpark. On many days, he would arrive early to carry a tee and a basket of balls to home plate. There, he would hit in solitude for about 30 minutes. Many nights, he would sign autographs before and after games. The moment he once couldn't imagine grew more obvious by the day.

"I come into ballparks with my eyes open a little wider. I try to take in all the things that maybe you take for granted that are pretty special moments," he said. "They could be dumb things like sitting on the bench by yourself and looking out

Cal tried to take in everything while making his last go-round of major league parks.

After disclosing his retirement plans on June 19, Ripken had a big July—a month in which he batted .368 with five home runs and 16 RBIs.

The End

over Fenway. There's a certain peace and feeling you have looking out on the field. Or it could be sitting in the clubhouse with a couple of guys."

As the season wound toward its conclusion, Ripken found his emotions intruding more on his renowned focus.

"I think there's a defense mechanism for my feelings and my emotions," Ripken said. "I've been pushing off the inevitable of the last anything. When I made the announcement early in the year, there was so much baseball ahead, so much to be enjoyed, that it was easy to push that away."

Ripken caught himself at Fenway Park during the first stop of his final road trip, but fought his emotions less effectively on the final leg at Yankee Stadium. Ripken became a historian of the game after overtaking Gehrig's streak, and the power of the game's most hallowed venue overtook him.

"It's not nervousness so much. It's probably what people go through when they get to the playoffs for the first time or the World Series for the first time. The excitement level goes up. The key is to contain it and to control it," said Ripken, who had hit what proved to be his last career home run against the Yankees on September 23 at Camden Yards. "It's not nervousness. I'm trained to do it. But it's difficult enough hitting the ball. If you can't contain your excitement and your energy, your timing is disturbed. There's more of a sense of urgency than before. You know your at-bats are limited, your games are limited. It's your last chance."

Ripken played in 3,001 major league games. He finished with a .276 career average in 11,511 at-bats, fourth-most in history.

Against the backdrop of such massive numbers, Ripken's difficult September represented merely a flyspeck, though it may have served to confirm the timing of his exit. He finished in a 2-for-48 slump, the most profound skid of his career. The drought dropped his season

Ovations were plentiful for Ripken during the countdown to retirement, and none was more emotional than the one he received on a ceremonial ride around Camden Yards (left) on the night of his final game.

average from .261 to .239; however, it barely lowered his career figure, from .276623 on September 25 to .275647 at year's end.

"I know he's probably going to be relieved when it's over," said outfielder Brady Anderson, Ripken's close friend and teammate since 1988. "A lot of athletes, when they leave, you feel bad for them. They seem so sad, distraught or devastated. It seems the opposite for Cal. I honestly think it's going to be a relief from the grind and the attention he has received. In that way, it won't be sad."

As a going-away gift, Ripken would have loved one more at-bat. In the ninth inning of that October 6 game, he saw a final chance approaching. If only Anderson could reach base with two outs.

"Do you want to hit again?" Anderson asked him before leaving the dugout.

"Yeah," Ripken answered, as if stating the obvious.

"OK, I'll make sure that happens," assured Anderson, not knowing that he

The End

had just assumed what Ripken later called "the most pressurized at-bat ever."

Batting seventh in the lineup, Ripken was stranded on deck when Anderson struck out against Red Sox reliever Ugueth Urbina. Sensing the finality of what it witnessed, the Camden Yards crowd cringed.

It was Ripken who consoled Anderson, saying only, "Let it go."

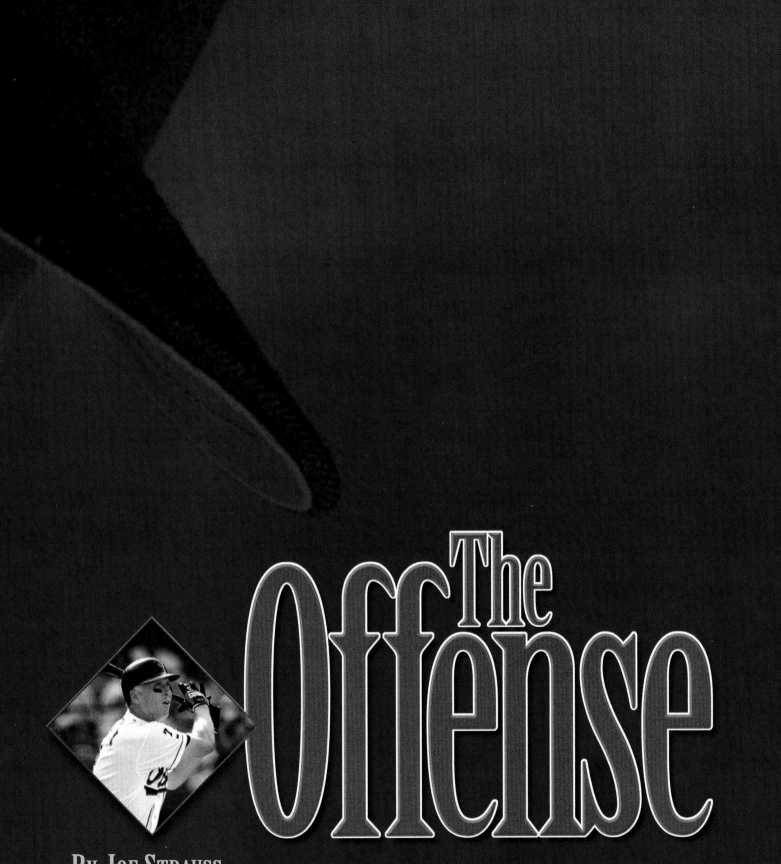

The Offense

By Joe Strauss

The Offense

Asked to summarize a prolific offensive career that occasionally touched brilliance but usually gravitated toward steady, grinding production, Cal Ripken might apply his philosophy regarding the myriad batting stances he employed during 21 major league seasons:

"For all the focus on what it looks like, the key component is your position at impact. It's about what puts you in the best position, nothing more and nothing less."

Ripken's legacy included redefinition of the shortstop position and, of course, a consecutive-game streak that most believe is truly unassailable. Strange, though, is that one of only seven players to amass 400 home runs and 3,000 hits carries a less-defined offensive image. Hall of Fame Orioles manager Earl Weaver wondered aloud early in Ripken's career whether the 6-4 infielder would develop into a home run or doubles hitter. Ripken's body of work suggests both; however, a year-by-year examination offers more complicated answers.

Ripken finished his career ranked in the all-time top 20 in at-bats, hits, RBIs, doubles and total bases and as the game's active RBI leader. He got there without a 35-homer or a 115-RBI season, thresholds that were major accomplishments in the majors at the beginning of his career but commonplace at its conclusion.

How Ripken got there involves a sometimes tortured journey. He persevered through the firing of his father as Orioles manager, overcame a midcareer crisis after winning his second Most Valuable Player award, steeled himself against a back condition that at first threatened his streak and then his

Despite a storied career that featured more than 400 home runs and 3,000 hits, Cal Ripken wasn't easy to define as an offensive player.

livelihood and managed a productive end to his career after being reunited with Terry Crowley, a former teammate turned hitting coach.

The outcome produced a record 345 home runs as a shortstop, 16 consecutive selections as an All-Star Game starter and a penchant for reviving his production whenever others rushed to detail its decline.

"Cal is a very good hitter because he is so good at making adjustments," Crowley said before Ripken's farewell season. "He watches and he understands what he sees. I've seen very few who could adjust as quickly as he does."

A man of 1,000 stances and more than 3,000 hits, Ripken wasn't as scientific a hitter as Tony Gwynn. But he was as determined a hitter as any who played during his era.

"I'm hard on young players. I want them to show me. But this kid really looks like he can play ... like he's destined," Crowley had said in 1981 when Ripken made his first appearance in a major league camp. (Crowley's own career was winding down at the time.)

Ripken reached 30 home runs once (1991), drove in 100 runs four times (1983, 1985, 1991, 1996) and never again scored 100 runs after doing so in three of his first four full seasons. But despite intermittently scalding and frustrating

The Offense

streaks, his overall consistency from year to year remained a marvel.

From 1982 through 1987, Ripken never hit more than 28 home runs nor fewer than 25. He drove in at least 80 runs in each of his first 10 seasons, amassing at least 90 RBIs in six of those years. By 1983, noted numbers guru Bill James was willing to anoint Ripken the game's best player.

Partly a function of his amazing durability, Ripken's numbers never rose exponentially but rather like compounded interest, piling atop one another until his consistency had created a mountain of production. When he singled off Minnesota Twins reliever Hector Carrasco in the seventh

Early in the 2000 season, Cal Ripken collected his 3,000th hit in a game at Minnesota and was congratulated by his wife, Kelly. The year before, he reached another milestone when he smashed his 400th home run (opposite page).

inning of a April 15, 2000, game, Ripken joined Hank Aaron, Willie Mays, Eddie Murray, Stan Musial, Dave Winfield and Carl Yastrzemski as the only players in the game's history to reach 400 home runs and 3,000 hits.

Ripken could be a riddle to managers and hitting coaches unable to penetrate his zone of trust. But, when hot, he was equally inscrutable to opposing pitchers. Brushing Ripken off the plate, knocking him down or hitting him only fueled his production. Even in the autumn of his career, Ripken remembered a beaning by Mike Moore as perhaps the most inspiring moment of his career. "A blessing in disguise," Ripken said of the incident, which occurred in his rookie season of

1982. "It was like swinging on a lever. Everything began to turn around. After getting beaned, I felt I really had something to prove."

His formative years were entrusted to his father, Cal Ripken Sr., the Orioles' longtime third base coach who served as the team's manager in 1987 and briefly in 1988. After the elder Ripken's departure from the organization in 1993, Ripken adopted a personalized pre-game routine that allowed for no wasted time. Tee work and flip drills were sandwiched around batting practice and infield. A watch was as important to his routine as a batting glove. So obsessed was he with punctuality that Ripken would often carry a case of several timepieces on road trips.

Ripken endured a tough summer in 1987, causing him to compare his hitting problems with the first month of his rookie season and general manager Hank Peters to ponder the pressure associated with playing more than 8,000

Brushing him off the plate, knocking him down or hitting him only fueled Ripken's production.

consecutive innings. "It's to the point with Ripken where he has to initiate (sitting)," Peters said. "He has to give a lot of thought to it. He has to talk to the guys who played this game a long time and get their thoughts on the pros and cons."

Finally, his father sat him in the eighth inning of a September 14 game, after Ripken had played 8,243 consecutive innings, a span of more than five seasons.

If 1987 was difficult, the next season was almost unbearable. Ripken's toughest stretch may have coincided with his father's ouster as manager. The son began the season in a 2-for-30 funk and was hitting .209 on June 13. For one of the few times in his career, Ripken heard boos—what Baltimore columnist John Steadman called a "dastardly humiliation."

Ripken salvaged a respectable season in 1988 (23 home runs, 81 RBIs) while drawing 100 walks for the only time his career. Yet he experienced another malaise in 1989, going 163 at-bats without a home run before recovering for 21 homers and 93 RBIs.

In 1990, Ripken's average fell to .250, lowest of his career. With his father coaching third base, Ripken chose not to seek out hitting coach Tom McCraw and his Hall of Fame manager, Frank Robinson.

"It's like walking down the street looking for an address. You keep getting that wrong address, but eventually you've got to go to the right door," Frank Robinson said at the time. "Right now, I don't see Cal adjusting. Everywhere I go, people say, 'I saw Ripken. He looks imbalanced. He's struggling.'"

Ripken wasn't immune to slumps late in his career, as his reflective mood and questioning looks (below) indicated. But nothing was quite like the 1988 season, when he got off to a 2-for-30 start at the plate and endured the "dastardly humiliation" of being booed during his batting funk.

Several frustrating years finally forced Ripken to seek outside assistance. At one point, he asked Robinson whether he was lunging toward the pitcher. "No," Robinson quipped. "You're sprinting at him. It looks like you're trying to run to the mound to get the ball out of the pitcher's hand."

After four seasons in which he failed to hit .270 and only once hit 25 home runs, Ripken enjoyed an offensive rebirth in 1991, setting career highs in home

runs (34) and RBIs (114) and collecting 210 hits, including a major league-high 85 for extra bases. His home runs were the most by a shortstop in 22 years and most by an Oriole since Ken Singleton in 1979.

Years later, Ripken would remember the season as a "magical" one for him when he again became comfortable at the plate while avoiding the lengthy slumps that hampered him the previous four seasons.

Ripken's batting average fluctuated wildly from 1990 to 1995, jumping 73 points in 1991 and then dropping 72 the next, as questions about The Streak's toll again sprouted. ("Maybe he's at the point in his career where he's not going to hit home runs anymore," Baltimore manager Johnny Oates said.)

Ripken experienced another spike in average in the strike-shortened 1994 season, when he batted .315—his second-highest figure since 1983—only one year after laboring to hit .257. Not until the winter of his career (1995 on) did Ripken's batting average maintain a steady level from year to year, as he batted from .256 to .278 with the exception of his abbreviated but magical .340 in 1999.

The patient hitter of the early 1980s grew into a voracious first-pitch swinger late in his career. Ripken walked more than 85 times only once in his career (1988) after virtually refusing to offer at a first pitch in his first several seasons. Approaching the end of his career, Ripken thought his best chance to cause damage came earlier in counts. He walked only 36 times in 1999-2000 while

A patient hitter at the beginning of his career, Ripken later changed his approach and began attacking first-pitch offerings. In 641 at-bats over the 1999 and 2000 seasons, he walked only 36 times while hitting 33 home runs.

The Offense

Part of a lusty-hitting lineup that included Rafael Palmeiro and Roberto Alomar (background), Ripken enjoyed his last big power season in 1996, a year in which he contributed 26 homers and 102 RBIs.

hitting 33 home runs in the same span.

One thread connecting both eras was Ripken's willingness to tinker with his stance. A closed setup, a deep crouch, a bat laid horizontally on his right shoulder and a high-handed waggle alternately became Ripken's signatures. No change was made capriciously; indeed, some followed protracted bouts of stubbornness.

Like many hitters, Ripken began making noticeable adjustments in his early 30s. He was partly prompted by a difficult 1992 season in which he failed to reach 20 home runs and 80 RBIs for the first time in his career.

"When you get frustrated, you can't be afraid to change your mechanics to get you to the point where your natural ability takes over," Ripken said. "That's something I forgot somewhere along the way."

As Robinson once noted: "There's no such thing as a bad stance, just bad results. There are a lot of unusual stances out there. If someone can hit a certain way, that's fine."

Ripken's stance became a constant work in progress. He would disappear from the clubhouse in October, retreat to his suburban Baltimore home and indoor batting cage, then return to Florida the next February with a newfangled setup. He disliked scrutiny of his various stances almost as much as criticism of The Streak. He considered both private possessions and always wondered about the motivation of inquiries into each.

"Cal feels—like most good hitters—that he knows himself better than anyone else," said teammate and Hall of Fame pitcher Jim Palmer. "Sometimes, the more outside advice you take, the worse off you're going to be. He will try to figure things out himself first, then start listening to people. When he does look for help, he looks to the people that know him the best. That's why he always went to his dad."

Ripken enjoyed another offensive reawakening in 1996, when the Orioles made their first postseason appearance in 13 seasons. Within a lineup that generated at least 20 home runs from Chris Hoiles, Brady Anderson, Roberto Alomar, B.J. Surhoff, Rafael Palmeiro and Bobby Bonilla, Ripken contributed 26 homers and 102 RBIs.

◆ ◆ ◆

The Streak lived through 1997, but just barely. Ripken began to have back spasms in July, and he never got complete relief through the rest of the team's wire-to-wire rush to its first A.L. East title since 1983. Again, criticism surfaced over Ripken's refusal to leave the lineup. Again, Ripken rebutted critics with 15 hits in the Orioles' 10 postseason games. But his October surge didn't allow him to escape a trying 1998.

In '98, Ripken adopted an exaggerated kick with his left leg to prevent himself from lunging at pitches. He offered no description for the unconventional stance but hardly approved when a beat reporter asked him about his "flamingo" step. Such characterizations, Ripken said, only minimized his purpose and the effort he devoted to cheating time.

"His hands are the only things that keep him alive," said Rick Down, the

Ripken's back problems flared in 1997, and criticism resurfaced over his refusal to leave the lineup. But Cal silenced many critics with 15 hits in 10 postseason games. In 1999, Ripken showed improved bat speed, thanks in large measure to a reunion with Terry Crowley (below, right), a former teammate-turned-batting coach.

"There have been times when you question yourself about whether it's worth it. Then there are those times when your body allows you to play a game you love to your capabilities. You don't want to miss that."

—Cal Ripken

Ripken was hurting for much of the '99 season—he had two stints on the D.L. before undergoing surgery in September—but nevertheless found a "magic swing" and hit .340 in 332 at-bats.

Orioles' hitting coach from 1996 through 1998, when Ripken's back problems first flared.

Early in his career, Ripken would seek the counsel of his father and one-time manager. Reunited with his old teammate, Crowley, in 1999, Ripken rediscovered a sense of trust with the Orioles' former pinch hitter extraordinaire.

Ripken's reunion with Crowley coincided with a return in his bat speed. Crowley persuaded Ripken to trust his body despite its various aches.

"The older a player gets, the more he becomes concerned with getting jammed," Crowley said. "To protect against that, a lot of players give something else away, whether it be reacting to a breaking ball or plate coverage."

Ripken initially adopted an exaggerated closed stance in 1999 as his lower back tormented him throughout the season. His problem, which forced him from the opening-day lineup after a brief appearance, was diagnosed as stenosis, an inflammation of nerves caused by a too-narrow canal from a vertebra in his back. The condition caused numbness and even a slight atrophying of his left leg. To compensate, Ripken would often jangle the leg while in the field and extend it in

The Offense

his stance at the plate. Twisting his trunk became difficult at times.

Somewhere within his painful 1999 season, Ripken found what he called a "magic swing." True, he endured two stays on the disabled list before finally undergoing season-ending surgery in September. But the intervening periods offered him some of his most productive streaks in years.

Ripken discarded his exaggerated stances for a more athletic-looking position in which he flexed both knees. His bat speed and confidence returned as his relationship with Crowley solidified.

Rather than rush himself, Ripken again waited with his hands and, in his abbreviated 1999 and 2000 seasons, drove in 113 runs in a combined 641 at-bats. If combined into a single season, the production would have represented the second-best year of his career.

"It's been a strange time," Ripken said. "There have been times when you question yourself about whether it's worth it. Then there are those times when your body allows you to play a game you love to your capabilities. You don't want to miss that."

Ripken played for nine managers in his 21 seasons with the Orioles. His next-to-last field boss was Ray Miller (below), who led the club in 1998 and '99 before giving way to Mike Hargrove.

The Streak

By
Peter Schmuck

The Streak

They build their legends to last in New York, where baseball truly became the national pastime in the days of Babe Ruth and Lou Gehrig, so no one thought it was particularly presumptuous to inscribe the Yankee Stadium monument honoring the Iron Horse with a tribute that was intended to remain veritable forever.

It's still there, testifying to Gehrig's greatness in Monument Park behind left field, but it is now slightly dated:

"Henry Louis Gehrig ... a man, a gentleman and a great ballplayer whose amazing record of 2,130 consecutive games should stand for all time. ..."

Who could have imagined that anyone would come along and challenge the Iron Horse? The record was so impressive, so far beyond what anyone had done before, that the Yankees were not unreasonable to assume that it would never be broken.

Think about it. Gehrig appeared in 2,130 consecutive games, which worked out to nearly 14 seasons without a break. Gehrig surpassed the previous record of 1,307—held by Red Sox/Yankees shortstop Everett Scott—in 1933, almost six years before the first baseman was forced out of the Yankees' lineup by the mysterious and fatal disease that now bears his name.

Over the next four decades, the most significant challenge to the record came from Steve Garvey, the Dodgers' and Padres' first baseman who set the National League record by playing in 1,207 straight games before a hand injury forced him to sit down in 1983. Garvey dreamed of going after Gehrig, but that dream died in a crash at home plate at about the time an infielder from Aberdeen, Md., was stepping

Lou Gehrig's mark seemed certain to stand the test of time, but then an infielder from Aberdeen, Md., came along.

Cal Ripken didn't mind meeting with the media, but he was reluctant to talk about The Streak.

The Streak

into the spotlight in Baltimore.

Cal Ripken arrived in the Orioles' everyday lineup in 1982 and would carve out a place in the national consciousness with an MVP performance that led the Orioles to a World Series championship in 1983. Nobody really thought much about May 30, 1982, back then. It would be several years before anyone began making reference to the first game of The Streak.

Certainly not Ripken, who was reluctant to acknowledge The Streak even as it headed toward 2,000 games. He shied away from interviews on the subject, denied any driving desire to challenge the record and resisted any temptation to read books about Gehrig—gifts from well-meaning friends and admirers—that were piling up around his home.

"My general response is to downplay it," he said as he opened the historic 1995 season with 2,009 consecutive games played. "You know I try not to give myself any level of importance, especially when it comes to that. I try to make it as simple as possible. I basically just go out and play because I want to go out there and play. I want to be in the lineup.

"My career has allowed me to stay in the lineup, and I've been lucky to stay away from any injuries. You know I don't make as big a deal as some other people make of it, and maybe that's the only way I can deal with it, the only way I can protect myself against changing my approach."

If Ripken inadvertently created the impression that acknowledging the quest might somehow jinx it, that wasn't it at all. Ripken shied away from focusing on The Streak because he felt that the public's growing fixation with it missed the point. He insisted over and over that the record chase was just a byproduct of his desire to play and to be a dependable teammate.

Ripken didn't just show up. He played every inning of every game from June 5, 1982, to the eighth inning of a September 14, 1987, game, a streak of 8,243 innings that is believed to be a major league record. He would have kept playing every inning of every game, but Orioles manager Cal Ripken Sr. removed him from a blowout game in Toronto out of concern that the innings streak might become counterproductive.

Through it all, Ripken did nothing to cheapen his greatest accomplishment. He started every game of The Streak and survived a number of threats to his legendary durability.

The Streak nearly ended before it became newsworthy when Ripken suffered a severe ankle sprain in his 444th consecutive game on April 10, 1985, but he missed only an exhibition game against the U.S. Naval Academy and was back in the lineup for the next game on the regular schedule.

Ripken sprained an ankle again during his 1,713th straight game in 1992, and he was hurt badly enough for the Orioles to recall reserve shortstop Manny Alexander from Class AAA Rochester as a precaution, but not badly enough to miss an inning over the next week.

The most serious threat to The Streak was a freak knee injury

> **If Ripken inadvertently created the impression that acknowledging the quest might somehow jinx it, that wasn't it at all. ... He insisted over and over that the record chase was just a byproduct of his desire to play and to be a dependable teammate.**

Ripken didn't just show up during The Streak. Despite getting battered and bruised throughout his odyssey to surpass Lou Gehrig's record, Ripken played in 8,243 consecutive innings in one stretch.

suffered during a brawl between the Orioles and Seattle Mariners on June 6, 1993. Ripken caught his spikes in the infield grass and twisted the knee so badly that he was considered doubtful for consecutive game No. 1,791. That morning, Ripken told his wife, Kelly, that he didn't believe he would be able to play, but the soreness and swelling subsided enough for The Streak to go on.

There was one other point when The Streak was in doubt, and it would turn out to be a harbinger of the eventual end of his career. Ripken already had broken Gehrig's record when a lower back injury nearly drove him out of the lineup in 1997, but he played on until the final days of the 1998 season.

The back problem would force Ripken out of the lineup for extended periods in 1999—he appeared in only 86 games—and it eventually forced him to retire.

Though Ripken periodically faced criticism for his stubborn desire to be in the lineup every day—regardless of its impact on his overall performance—he never did anything strictly for The Streak. He never left a game intentionally in the early innings. He never asked for a day in the designated hitter role.

Even Gehrig cut a few corners to keep his streak alive. Twice while he was battling injuries, Gehrig appeared in games as the leadoff hitter and was removed after his first at-bat. He also missed two starts during the first year of his streak and played every inning of every game in only one season. Of course, Ripken would admit to knowing nothing about Gehrig as he closed in on the record in 1995.

"Everyone makes the natural assumption that I want to know about Lou Gehrig, that there's maybe some obsession with Lou Gehrig," Ripken said.

"I'm curious now because it's been brought up so many times. But, the way I protect myself is to not know anything about him, because I did not set out to do this.

"I'm not chasing Lou Gehrig. I'm just going out there and being myself and

trying to play the way I was brought up to play. So I have a couple books that were given to me. And I have some articles that were given to me. But I just put them away in a safe place. Maybe after this is all said and done one way or the other, my curiosity will get the better of me and I'll be able to read about it."

Comparisons with Gehrig aren't worthwhile anyway. The Iron Horse was one of the greatest offensive players in the history of the sport. Ripken was the prototype for the crop of big-hitting shortstops that came along in the 1990s, but only in a couple of seasons (1983 and 1991) was he one of the American League's dominant hitters.

He produced big numbers in relation to the position he played—and would be a first-ballot Hall of Famer even without The Streak—but it was his all-around performance that made Ripken one of the game's true all-time greats.

"The only comparison you can make between me as a player and Lou Gehrig as a player is that we have the streak in common," Ripken said. "Other than that, he was a far better hitter than I'll ever be, probably a far better player than I'll ever be."

Maybe he didn't hit like Gehrig, but Ripken played a far more demanding position than the legendary Yankees first baseman. He put himself in harm's way to turn thousands of double plays and still was durable enough to tack 502 games onto Gehrig's supposedly unbreakable consecutive-games record.

Not, however, before The Streak would face a threat more dangerous than a dozen home-plate crashes—baseball's fractious labor situation. The plan by baseball owners to employ replacement players to open the 1995 season put Ripken's record chase in serious danger, because he had made it clear that he would not cross a picket line to keep The Streak alive.

No one knows if the owners really intended to go through with the replacement strategy, but they ran into a roadblock when Orioles owner Peter

Ripken produced impressive numbers in relation to the position he played—and it didn't hurt that he kept himself in shape so he could muscle up at the plate.

The Streak

Angelos refused to field a replacement team. Angelos, who cut his teeth as a lawyer representing labor unions, stood firm against the plan to assure that Ripken's streak would not be endangered.

The owners eventually backed away from the replacement strategy and the labor dispute was settled in time to play most of the 1995 schedule, but the protracted strike cost baseball more than two months of regular-season play and forced the cancellation of the 1994 World Series. If not for the labor war, Ripken would have broken Gehrig's record in June instead of September in 1995.

Ripken doesn't even like to talk about what might have happened if the replacement scheme had gone into effect. He stood firm with the union, even though many union members publicly encouraged him to cross the picket line and keep The Streak alive.

"I think some of that was blown out of proportion," Ripken said at the time.

Ripken played a far more demanding position than Gehrig did. He also endured something the Hall of Fame first baseman never encountered—a fractious labor situation.

"I don't think some of that was ever said. I don't know how true those stories ever were. Obviously it would've made me feel good (that someone would say that), but it would never happen. I'm a big-league baseball player, and if there's big-league baseball, then I'll be playing.

"I try not to worry about things I can't control, and I honestly didn't worry too much about that."

When the strike finally ended, Ripken was faced with a new challenge. The season of his record-breaking moment also would be the first season after the most damaging and disillusioning work stoppage in the history of professional sports.

Baseball had been dealt a severe blow to its credibility, and it would be up to the players to reach out to fans—many of whom were too disgusted to return to the ballpark.

Ripken, the guy with the milk moustache and the amazing work ethic, was the logical choice to breach that wall of fan resentment and rebuild the image of the troubled industry. He accepted the challenge without even being asked.

Never comfortable with public adulation or media scrutiny, he spoke into every microphone and filled every notebook through the final spring and summer of his record pursuit.

And he did something else that sealed the deal with the game's disenchanted clientele. He stayed after games—sometimes for hours—signing autographs for thousands of fans at Camden Yards and on the club's road stops.

It seemed as if Ripken spoke into every microphone, signed every autograph and filled every notebook through the final spring and summer of his record pursuit.

They would start queuing up near the Orioles' dugout in the eighth inning, the lines sometimes stretching hundreds of feet. It became such a distraction for the fans in the field boxes in Baltimore that the Orioles finally had to ask Ripken to end the postgame sessions at Camden Yards.

The added responsibility had to make the final months of the record chase that much more difficult, but Ripken carried it off with a grace and style that endeared him to an entire generation of baseball fans.

After so many years of sidestepping questions about Gehrig and The Streak, Cal Ripken finally embraced it and joined the Iron Horse in the annals of baseball history.

On September 5, 1995, he played in his 2,130th consecutive game to tie the record and evoke an unprecedented outpouring of emotion from the sellout crowd at Oriole Park.

Ripken tied Gehrig's record of playing in 2,130 consecutive games on the night of September 5, 1995—and he spiced the festive evening with a home run (above).

On September 6, the record that was supposed to stand for all time fell when Ripken took his position in the field in the middle of the fifth inning. Fireworks exploded over Camden Yards. The countdown (actually, it was a count-up) on the wall of the B&O warehouse reached 2,131. The ovation lasted longer than some innings.

Ripken, teary-eyed and overwhelmed, went to the stands to greet his family, waved to his beaming parents, then took an unexpected victory lap around the stadium, shaking hands and high-fiving fans in a spontaneous burst of mutual affection that turned the evening into an all-American lovefest.

The new reigning iron man, whose usually steely emotions were stretched to their limit, was pushed out of the dugout by teammates Bobby Bonilla and Rafael Palmeiro for the jog around Camden Yards. Only in a little big town like

When Ripken connected for another homer in record-setting game No. 2,131 (above), it meant he had risen to the occasion—again.

Baltimore could it have had such meaning, with Ripken seeing familiar faces all along the route.

Even the Angels, who would fall victim to his heroics—Ripken hit a home run in both the record-tying and record-breaking games—lined up on the dugout steps to shake his hand. His accomplishment transcended the color of his uniform and repaired the jagged tear that baseball's labor war had left in the fabric of the sport.

There weren't a lot of dry eyes in Baltimore that night. Hall of Famer Joe DiMaggio, who played with Gehrig in the 1930s, was overcome with emotion.

Owner Peter Angelos took the podium after the game and pledged $2 million

Ripken's accomplishment transcended the color of his uniform and repaired the jagged tear that baseball's labor war had left in the fabric of the sport.

to fund research to find a cure for Lou Gehrig's disease. The fans wanted to stay all night.

That one enchanted evening cemented Ripken's Hall of Fame credentials, though his record for home runs by a shortstop and his 3,000th hit would make him an all-but-automatic first-ballot entrant even without The Streak.

No doubt, the wave of emotion that enveloped Ripken on September 6 soon gave way to a wave of relief. The Streak would go on for three more years, but Ripken would no longer have to defend it.

The quest had drawn criticism as early as 1989, when Ripken's numbers tailed off at the end of an exciting season in which the Orioles wound up two games out of first place. His struggles in September over several seasons prompted speculation that The Streak was eroding his energy late in the season, but Ripken did something in 1991 that took that issue off the table for several years.

He turned in the best offensive season of his career in '91, batting .323 with 34 home runs and 114 RBIs, and he maintained a high level of production right through September. The fatigue issue faded away until after Ripken broke the record in 1995. It would not rise again until after Ripken sat down in 1998, and only as a postscript to The Streak, because Ripken's offensive numbers turned upward between stays on the disabled list in 1999.

The Streak finally ended on September 20, 1998—and, happily, it ended entirely on Ripken's terms. He had struggled with back soreness the season before, but no physical limitation caused him to walk into manager Ray Miller's office just 20 minutes before the first pitch and ask for his name to be removed from the lineup card for a game against the Yankees.

It simply was the right time. Prospect Ryan Minor started at third base, and

After galloping past the Iron Horse, Cal brought his parents onto the field to share in the glory of his landmark achievement.

The Streak

Ripken's streak went into the record book at 2,632. To put it in further perspective, the 501 consecutive games that Ripken played after breaking Gehrig's record would have been the longest active streak in major league baseball at the time and was 38 games longer than the second-longest playing streak in Orioles history (463, Brooks Robinson).

Ripken wanted little fanfare. He simply sat out one game and then returned to the lineup to play the final seven games of the season. The Streak would define him, but it also would stand as a lasting tribute to the work ethic preached by Cal Ripken Sr.—not just to his sons, but also to hundreds of Orioles players over the previous 40 years.

"My approach to the game has probably been influenced most by my father," Ripken said. "Essentially, in a team game like baseball, your teammates rely on you to be in the lineup everyday. From the very beginning, my dad preached that it was important to be there, in the lineup, on a daily basis. Maybe I've exaggerated the point a little bit, but I still think it's important to go out there and play 162 games.

"Whether you play 140 or 120 games, there will always be days when you

Ripken acknowledged an ovation from Baltimore fans on September 20, 1998, shortly after the crowd learned that Cal had asked manager Ray Miller to remove his name from the lineup card. By sitting out the Sunday night game against the Yankees, Ripken saw his playing streak end at 2,632 games.

feel 70 percent. But there's always something you can do in the course of a game. That is the beauty of baseball. ... It's just always been preached to me to be out there and in the lineup everyday. My father is the one that turned me in that direction."

The debate over the advisability of The Streak—in terms of its effect on Ripken's day-to-day performance—will never be settled. Ripken set a standard for offensive production from the shortstop position and will go into the Hall of Fame with outstanding cumulative numbers, but there will always be room to wonder what his statistics might have been if he had allowed himself a few days off.

His sterling performance during a 1999 season interrupted several times by painful back problems—he batted .340 with 18 home runs in 332 at-bats—suggest that he might have been a more efficient offensive player if he had not insisted on such a grueling schedule, but who cares?

The Streak became a national treasure, and Ripken became the white knight who saved baseball from its own self-destructive tendencies. What could be better than that?

Miller, who deleted Ripken's name from the lineup (above) and wrote in Ryan Minor as Cal's replacement, embraced baseball's iron man at game's end. Although it simply was the right time for Ripken to end his streak, Cal was back on the job for Baltimore in the Orioles' final seven games of the '98 season.

The Streak

The Stage

By
MICHAEL KNISLEY

When Cal Ripken (with his wife and daughter) toasted his banner 1991 season, the beverage of choice was—no big surprise here—milk.

The Stage

This is so ... so *Cal*.

There he is, standing in the early-evening chill of November 19, 1991, in the box seats at a yet-to-be-opened Oriole Park at Camden Yards, and he's making a toast in a champagne glass. The occasion is his second Most Valuable Player award.

In the glass? No, that isn't champagne. Champagne would be so *not Cal*.

It's milk.

This is how he celebrates the best season of his career. At a news conference in his honor, in front of the Baltimore media shortly after the results of the American League's MVP voting have been announced, in a ballpark built for him, a ballpark built around him as a monument to baseball's bygone days, Cal drinks a glass of milk.

It's perfect.

And why not? The 1991 season, for all intents and purposes save one, was the milk of a new life, or at least a lease on a new life, for Ripken. He hit .323, the highest batting average of his career for a full season. He hit 34 home runs, more than in any other of his 20 seasons. He drove in 114 runs, also a career high. He led the majors in extra-base hits with 85, in total bases with 368 and in multi-hit games with 73.

In November 1991, Ripken was halfway through his two decades as a player, on a team in transition from Memorial Stadium to Camden Yards. If the previous four seasons, during which he had averaged *only* 23 home runs and 89 RBIs and didn't hit higher than .264, had created doubts that he could regain the promise and productivity of his first few years in the league, then 1991 put them to rest, emphatically. He was brilliant.

The Stage

As he stood in front of a battery of microphones that night, he said, "I always assumed I was going to have a long career. But last year I thought, 'Maybe it's not going to be that long. Maybe my days are numbered.' "

The days of '91, instead, were chock full of all the right numbers, including defensive numbers. Ripken led all American League shortstops in every key defensive statistical category in '91. He was first in fielding percentage (.986), putouts (267), assists (528), chances (806) and double plays (114).

A year earlier, he had established himself firmly as one of the game's all-time best defensive shortstops when he played 161 games and committed only three errors—*three!* But in '91, he put the offense together with his defense. His game had never been so complete.

"It was a storybook season," he said that November night at Camden Yards. "It seemed like whenever I was out there on the field, I could do no wrong. Very rarely do you get that feeling as an athlete."

The one purpose, the only purpose, not served by Ripken's '91 season was the Orioles' record. The team was terrible. It wound up next to last in the seven-team A.L. East, going 67-95 and finishing 24 games out of first place. But the Orioles' failure made Ripken's success even more remarkable. Never before in the

American League had a player on a team with a losing record been named MVP, and it had happened in the National League only three times.

Against that summer of dreariness, Ripken dazzled. Not only was he the first A.L. player to win the Most Valuable Player award on a sub-.500 team, he also was named Major League Player of the Year by both *The Sporting News* and The Associated Press. And he was selected MVP of the 1991 All-Star Game after hitting a three-run home run off Dennis Martinez and a single against Tom Glavine in the American League's 4-2 victory at Toronto's SkyDome. (The day before the All-Star Game, Ripken was the star of the home run contest. He clubbed 12 homers in 22 swings to lead the A.L. to a 20-7 triumph in that exhibition.)

Oh, and he won his first Gold Glove in 1991, too. If all of that isn't worth a milk mustache on a cold November night, what is?

"He was very consistent from opening day until the end of the season," said Frank Robinson, who began '91 as the Orioles' manager and finished it as an assistant general manager. "It was even more amazing because we had no one in the lineup to protect him."

If one season in Ripken's marvelous career pinpoints his emergence as a national baseball icon—the consecutive-games streak aside—it was 1991.

The Streak was one thing. Cal's consummate talent, which is what made The Streak possible in the first place, was another. The 1991 season made him, once and for all, so much more than just a player who played every day.

Inside baseball, that year made his game ... well, unimpeachable.

"I think the great players reach a time in their careers when other players respect them," said Johnny Oates, Ripken's manager in Baltimore from early in 1991 through 1994. "I know I did it, and I'm sure most players do. Guys like Alan Trammell or maybe a guy like George Brett reach a point where they start getting that kind of respect. Players know who those guys are."

In '91, Cal Ripken reached that point.

In '92, with the opening of Camden Yards, his reach extended far beyond the

The Stage

respect of baseball insiders.

Ten years into his career, Cal was a well-established favorite son in Baltimore, and it was as much for his integrity as for his play. That glass of milk was no accident that November night. He was a spokesperson for the Mid-Atlantic Milk Marketing Association, a regional endorsement opportunity chosen precisely because it so perfectly fit his wholesome image. In Baltimore, Cal already was recognized as a throwback, his steady play and unassailable work ethic a constant reminder of the roll-up-the-sleeves tradition on which America and America's national pastime were forged.

Now, the rest of the world was taking notice of the quality of his character. In 1992, he was presented the Roberto Clemente Award as the player who best

Great players eventually win the utmost respect of their peers. Cal reached that level in 1991.

Ripken got a lot from baseball—but he gave a lot back, too, as his many off-the-field endeavors proved. After helping to create the Ripken Learning Center in 1988, he made a $250,000 contribution to the adult literacy program in 1997 and met with grateful students and staff (immediate right). Ripken's role-model deeds grew larger when, in 1992, the Orioles moved to a perfect stage, Camden Yards, over which Ripken still ruled at decade's end (opposite page).

exemplified baseball on and off the field. That year, he won the Lou Gehrig Memorial Award, too, which is given by the Phi Delta Theta national collegiate fraternity to the major leaguer who best fits the image and manner of their fraternity brother, the Hall of Fame first baseman whose consecutive-games record Ripken would break three years later.

Eventually, Ripken would have become a national idol anyway, as he inexorably approached Gehrig's record. But when the Orioles moved into Camden Yards in April 1992, that process ratcheted up to warp speed.

It's easy to forget, now that so many ballparks have imitated it, that Camden Yards was the first new stadium to harken back consciously to the charm and intimacy of baseball's bygone era. It was built of arched brick facades and steel (not concrete) trusses. It had advertising on the outfield fence and the 95-year-old, red-brick B&O warehouse beyond right field. It was downtown, neatly assimilated into a skyline that still features a venerable Bromo Seltzer clock tower.

Camden Yards was brand new in '92, but it came furnished with built-in legends. Center field, for instance, is said to be the site of a saloon where Babe Ruth's father sold beer for a nickel and soup for a dime. The Babe himself supposedly learned the game of baseball on the nearby streets.

To those whose memories extend back that far, Camden Yards called forth the ghosts of Ebbets Field, Shibe Park, Crosley Field, Forbes Field, the Polo Grounds. Yet it also managed to set a new standard in stadium design for comfort

The Stage

At the 1997 season opener at Camden Yards, Orioles owner Peter Angelos and throwback player Ripken took in the sights at their throwback ballpark. Ripken then went out and hit two doubles and a home run as Baltimore defeated the Kansas City Royals.

The Stage

and technological creativity.

The effect was this: Now Baltimore had a present-day throwback ballpark to go with its present-day throwback hero. As Ripken provided a link to Gehrig, Camden Yards gave fans a connection to baseball's lost palaces. And as the stadium generated unprecedented excitement around the country, it was impossible to overlook the harmony and dignity of the marriage between Ripken and Camden Yards. Cal was becoming a role model to millions, and now he had the perfect stage on which to play that part.

The stadium immediately was a tourist attraction on a national scale, a high-tech, hands-on museum of baseball. With Ripken as its curator.

The new ballpark may not have been the House That Cal Built. But he was—in one way, at least—responsible for the way it was constructed. When the Orioles' design team drew up the new stadium's outfield dimensions, they researched Ripken's statistics in other ballparks around the country and found that he had hit better in Minnesota's Metrodome than anywhere else. Camden Yards fences then were made to approximate the Metrodome's dimensions.

Interestingly, though, Cal's game didn't take to Camden Yards immediately. His average fell to .251 in 1992 and .257 in 1993. During the '93 season, he said, "Memorial Stadium was a better fit for me than Camden Yards. This is a lot flashier place. I hope I'm not considered a flashy player." But by 1994, he was at

Camden Yards, which played host to the 1993 All-Star Game and the Home Run Derby that preceded it, may not have been the House That Cal Built, yet its configuration was based in large measure on Ripken's hitting tendencies.

The Stage

home, flashy or not. He hit .315 in that strike-shortened season.

There was something so right about Ripken in Camden Yards. That became evident to one and all on the night of July 13, 1993. Baltimore played host to the All-Star Game that evening, and the occasion served as a sort of debutante ball for the year-and-a-half-old park. Of course, Cal was the American League's starting shortstop.

It was a nationally televised lovefest. When longtime Baltimore broadcaster Chuck Thompson introduced Ripken before the game, the crowd erupted. The ovation went on and on, and might still be going if Thompson hadn't felt the need to push forward with the next man in the A.L. batting order. He broke in with, "Batting eighth, playing third base, from the New York Yankees, Wade Boggs."

It wasn't a popular move.

"Chuck interrupted them when they were cheering for Cal," said Orioles pitcher Mike Mussina, an All-Star himself. "They've been waiting 10 years for that. Cal earned it."

There would be many more memorable moments for Ripken in Camden Yards—certainly none as unforgettable as the night of September 6, 1995, the night he broke Gehrig's record. But it's instructive to remember the first one, the one with which this chapter began, that celebratory moment with a glass of milk in the brand new baseball cathedral called Oriole Park at Camden Yards, deserted

except for a handful of local writers and broadcasters, some Orioles team officials and a few hundred surprised passers-by who wandered in to see why the stadium lights were on.

From that point, from that first public appearance there, this paragon of wholesomeness—whose respect for the game's heritage was evident in every move he made—no longer belonged solely to the Baltimore Orioles.

From that moment on, Ripken belonged to all of us.

The Defense

By
PETER SCHMUCK

6

The Defense

Cal Ripken's offensive accomplishments brought immediate dividends. He was named the American League's Rookie of the Year in 1982 after hitting 28 home runs. He then was selected the American League's Most Valuable Player in his second full major league season, a year in which he batted .318 and drove in 102 runs.

In short order, Ripken emerged as the prototype for a new generation of power-hitting, run-producing shortstops.

It had to be richly rewarding to be recognized so quickly as one of the greatest offensive threats ever to play regularly at shortstop, but that came with a price. The Rookie of the Year and MVP voters may have factored in the difficult position he played, but it was clear that his solid defensive skills were being overshadowed by his performance at the plate.

Want proof?

From 1982 through 1990, Ripken led the American League in assists five times, putouts and double plays four times each and chances three times. He led all four categories in the same year twice, but he didn't win a single Gold Glove for fielding excellence.

The 1990 season was particularly difficult to overlook. Ripken set a major league record with 95 consecutive errorless games. He also established records for fewest errors in a season by a shortstop (three), highest fielding percentage (.996) and most consecutive chances (428) without an error, only to see the Gold Glove go to White Sox defensive specialist Ozzie Guillen.

The 1990 season was such a defensive tour de force that it seemed inconceivable American League

Throwing on the run while making a tough play proved old hat for Ripken, whose consistency afield was a hallmark of his career.

Ripken, who in 1989 led A.L. shortstops by taking part in 119 double plays, glides over the Indians' Joe Carter and makes the throw on to first base in action that season.

The Defense

coaches and managers (who vote for the Gold Glove) could overlook Ripken. Rangers manager Bobby Valentine was so shocked that he told reporters he was "embarrassed by the actions of my peers."

Ripken could see it coming. He was playing old-fashioned baseball in the Ozzie Smith era, making difficult plays look routine when the other stars at his position were doing back flips. Guillen made 17 errors, but he got credit for his superior range and, presumably, overt athleticism.

"I really didn't get my hopes up," Ripken said. "It's a vote of the coaches and managers, and, if I do my job right, I don't get noticed. That's just my style of play. My hopes weren't too high, but to be honest, I'd like to win one of those things."

Baltimore manager Frank Robinson wasn't surprised, either. Those who fill out ballots get to see a player 12 or 13 times a year. They're going to remember the memorable plays, not the consistent players.

"When managers and coaches vote on something like that, they don't look at statistics," Robinson said at the time. "They review players in their minds and determine who they think is best based on what they've seen. They don't see him every day, and I think Cal is one of those players you have to see every day in order to appreciate what he does.

"I see him every day, and it's mind-boggling what he's done this year. I played with (Mark) Belanger ... but to go out there every day and have only three errors ... is almost unbelievable."

In reality, the Gold Glove snub may have done more to put Ripken's defensive skills in the national spotlight than any of his accomplishments during his amazing 1990 season. They don't show routine plays on *SportsCenter*— certainly not 400 of them in a row—but they do like controversy.

Ever the soft-spoken politician, Ripken did not complain bitterly or blast the voters. He chose instead to focus on his performance as a step closer to the recognition he felt he deserved.

"I think with all the attention that my defense got with the errorless streak and the three errors all season, people's opinions are starting to change a little bit," he said. "But I don't think it has gotten me over the hump.

"For so many years, my offense has overshadowed my defense, and I'm happy that it has. I don't want my defense to overshadow my offense. But maybe it will take a few more errorless-game streaks for people to realize that I'm not just an offensive player."

There would be no more record errorless streaks, only the irony that it would take Ripken's greatest offensive season to gain him the ultimate recognition for his defensive performance.

Everything changed in 1991, when

> **"I played with (Mark) Belanger ... but to go out there every day and have only three errors ... is almost unbelievable."**
>
> —*Frank Robinson, on Ripken's 1990 season*

Ripken set career highs with a .323 average, 34 home runs and 114 RBIs. He would be named the American League's Most Valuable Player for the second time and would highlight the dream season with an MVP performance in the All-Star Game. He also would make 11 errors, the most he had made in three seasons, but voters finally took note of his steady performance and awarded him the first of two consecutive Gold Gloves.

Ripken led the league in fielding percentage, putouts, assists, chances and double plays. If Guillen exhibited better range in 1990, Ripken picked up the slack in '91. If Ripken made fewer errors in '90, he insisted that his overall performance was better in 1991.

The Defense

"I thought last year (1990) I was deserving of consideration," he said after learning that he had finally won his first Gold Glove, "but I don't evaluate myself on the number of errors I made. Even though I had the high fielding percentage and so few errors, I had difficulty last year anticipating. I didn't feel like I knew our pitchers that well. I didn't feel I was as good last year. This year, I felt better."

He would win the award again in 1992, but his growing offensive resume would continue to obscure his defensive accomplishments— especially outside Baltimore.

Trouble was, he just didn't overwhelm anyone with his great range and athletic ability—though he was unquestionably one of the best all-around athletes in the game. Slick-fielding shortstops such as Smith and Guillen had better range and greater flair, but Ripken made up for that with greater consistency and an uncanny ability to be in the right place at the right time.

"I once read a quote from Dallas Green where he said that probably the most important thing for a shortstop is to be a two-out shortstop," said former Ripken teammate and Hall of Famer Jim Palmer. "I asked him what he meant and he said, 'When there are two outs and it's hit to the shortstop, you know everybody's coming off the field. You know he's going to make the play he has to make.'"

Ripken's all-around defensive talent— which included throwing out runners from his knees (opposite page) and handling low throws (below)—inspired Orioles fans to honor him with a banner. Gold Glove voters got around to honoring him in 1991 and 1992.

No one positioned himself better at shortstop. No infielder was more aware of the tendencies of opposing hitters. Ripken didn't have to make a lot of diving plays because he had a knack for being there before the ball.

Ripken heard the whispers. He was too big. Too slow. Too third base. He would play along, joking that he was "big and slow and cumbersome." He was the biggest man ever to play shortstop on a regular basis in the major leagues, but

The Defense

"I once read a quote from Dallas Green, where he said that probably the most important thing for a shortstop is to be a two-out shortstop. ... When there are two outs and it's hit to the shortstop ... you know he's going to make the play."

—*Jim Palmer, on the kind of reliability demonstrated by Cal Ripken*

the rest of the objections didn't float.

"He was the first of his type," Palmer said. "Nobody played the position that tall. I just think that in baseball, traditionally the assumption was made that if you were that big and played shortstop, it was because of your bat."

Ripken actually was a pitching prospect in high school, but he came up through the Orioles' minor league system as a likely heir to his boyhood idol—Hall of Famer Brooks Robinson.

Even Mr. Oriole himself was impressed with the big third baseman who had grown up in the Orioles' organization and arrived in the major leagues to stay after veteran Doug DeCinces was traded to the Angels. "Cal is such a fine offensive player, I think his defense has been overlooked," Robinson said. "No one does it better."

Ripken played third only briefly before manager Earl Weaver decided to try him at shortstop. The rest, of course, is history. He redefined the role of the shortstop and created the prototype that would be copied by an entire generation of offensive stars at the position.

"The organization had thought he'd be a third baseman," Weaver said. "When you've got a guy who's going to hit 20-25 home runs and drive in 80 runs and

Ripken created the shortstop prototype that would be copied by a generation—a big man who could make all the plays in the field and excel with the bat as a run-producer.

The Defense

field the position, he's definitely shortstop material. It's as simple as that."

Weaver bucked organizational wisdom. The Orioles' front office wanted to develop shortstop prospect Bob Bonner and keep Ripken at third base, but Weaver would have none of it.

"Bobby Bonner was head and shoulders above Ripken as far as being a shortstop," Weaver said in a 1995 interview. "The organization said, 'We'll get Bonner to play shortstop and Ripken at third and we'll be set on the left side of the infield for years to come. Bobby had reached his peak (he was 26 in 1982), whereas Ripken was improving, improving, improving every year. Bobby Bonner didn't make it in the big leagues (he appeared in only 61 games over four years for Baltimore) and Ripken did.

"Whether I was there or not, I don't know if it would have gotten started. But I said that as long as I'm manager, that kid's name is going to be in the lineup at shortstop."

Ripken would play every day at the position for the next 14 years, transforming it into an offensive position while playing so well defensively that Weaver and the Orioles would never have reason to regret the controversial position change.

"Maybe he wasn't a true shortstop," Palmer said, "but I think there was a time

"Cal is such a
fine offensive
player, I think
his defense
has been
overlooked.
No one does it
better."

—*Brooks Robinson*

people assumed that Weaver would take any defensive liability to get offense, which wasn't the case. Obviously, he (Ripken) was underrated because people thought he was at shortstop for the wrong reasons. By the time Alex Rodriguez came along, it was acceptable."

Rodriguez could be headed for 500 home runs and 3,500 hits. Boston's Nomar Garciaparra has emerged as perhaps the best pure hitter in the sport. Yankees star Derek Jeter is one of the most exciting offensive players in either league.

They all point to Ripken as their role model, because he merged his great offensive talent with the strong defensive performance that made him indispensable in the middle of the infield. Only when he moved into his late 30s did it become necessary for him to move back to the position he once seemed destined to play.

Ripken's range at shortstop became a sensitive issue in the mid-'90s, when manager Davey Johnson approached him about an experiment at third base. The club needed to know whether promising reserve shortstop Manny Alexander was capable of playing regularly at the position.

After the '96 season, the Orioles signed defensive specialist Mike Bordick and moved Ripken to third base full time. ... The Orioles would spend every day of the 1997 season in first place.

Ripken reluctantly agreed to spend a few days at third base in 1996 before returning to his primary position. Though the speedy Alexander would prove only that he was correctly cast as a reserve player, the brief experiment would lead to a permanent position change for the greatest offensive shortstop in baseball history.

After the '96 season, the Orioles signed defensive specialist Mike Bordick and moved Ripken to third base full time. If he was unhappy about it, he didn't say anything publicly. It helped that he had great respect for the steady defensive skills of Bordick, a low-key player with a Ripken-like work ethic.

The transition was as smooth as anyone in the Orioles organization could have hoped. Ripken quickly adapted to third base and became one of the better defensive players at the position. Bordick fit right in at shortstop, combining with Roberto Alomar to form one of the best double-play combinations in either league. The infield—which also included big-hitting first baseman Rafael Palmeiro—was one of the most balanced and productive in the game. The Orioles would spend every day of the 1997 season in first place.

The position change only reinforced Ripken's reputation as an outstanding all-around athlete, but it also may have hastened the end of his career. The back problems that would hamper him in his final four seasons coincided with the switch to third, a position that requires far more sudden movements and puts more strain on the lower back.

Maybe it was just a coincidence, but Ripken struggled with back soreness late in the 1997 season and nearly had to end his record consecutive-games streak in August of that year. He would carry the streak to the final days of the 1998 season before voluntarily sitting out a game, but the back problem would force him to the sidelines three times in 1999 and continue to hamper him during the 2000 season.

Still, he remained a steady defensive performer at third base when he was healthy enough to go out there. His major league career, which had started at that position 18 years earlier, had come full circle.

The Defense

The position
change only
reinforced
Ripken's
reputation as
an outstanding
all-around
athlete, but it
also may have
hastened the
end of his
career.

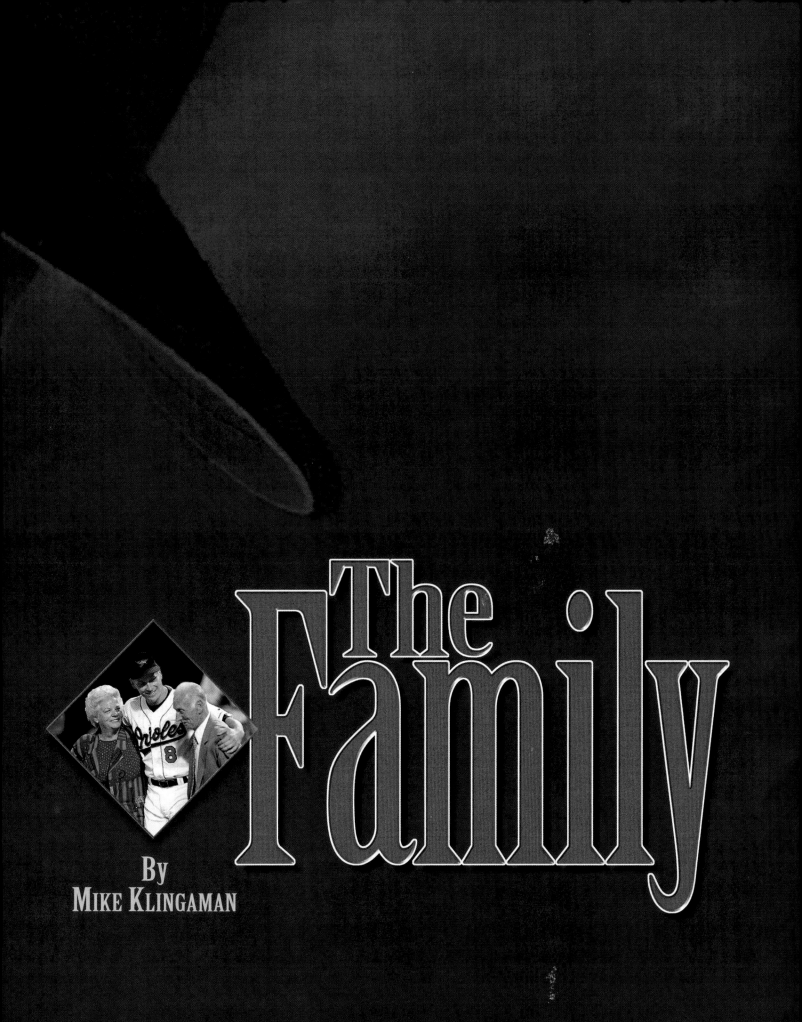

The Family

By
Mike Klingaman

The Family

It is the seminal snapshot of the Ripken era, more telling than the image of Cal basking in the glow of those incandescent numbers the night of his Gehrigian achievement.

Yes, the defining moment of Cal Ripken's career came earlier, in a 1987 photo shoot. There, beside the batting cage, stands baseball's first family: Cal, brother Bill and their father, Cal Sr.— the Orioles' new manager and the middle of his infield.

The sons are half-smirking, the kind of knowing look that siblings share when they've pulled a fast one. Their old man wears his patented somber visage—part American Gothic, part Eeyore. Fooled you. Inside, he is busting his orange-and-black buttons.

Never before had a big-league manager piloted two of his own simultaneously, as Cal Sr. did that season and part of the next.

The Pittsburgh Pirates of the late-'70s bragged, "We are fam-a-lee!"

The Orioles of the '80s had the DNA to prove it.

In 1987, Cal Jr. was 26, an All-Star shortstop with a million-dollar paycheck, MVP hardware and a milk mustache. He had a .289 career batting average, a World Series ring and an air of durability. "The streak" was still a babe—and lower case.

Bill, 22, was a rookie second baseman, an overachiever with deft hands, a puckish sense of humor and a cockeyed grin suggesting he had slid headfirst once too often.

Cal Sr. was patriarch of the clan. A tough, wiry bantam of a man, he had spent much of his sons' youth on the road, managing 14 years in the minors, preaching the Oriole Way in backwater towns from

The Ripken family portrait was a defining moment—a father, Cal Sr. (middle), managing two sons, Cal Jr. (right), and Bill, in the majors.

When the Class A Tri-City Atoms celebrated Father's Day in 1965, manager Cal Ripken Sr. was front and center with his children (left to right) Cal Jr., Fred, Bill and Elly.

The Family

the Dakotas to the Carolinas. Now, at 51, he found himself running the parent club and parenting it, too. "Rip" and kin, folks called them.

A cozier setting Cal Jr. could not imagine. Nor a more ironic one.

"Baseball took dad away from me when I was growing up," he said in 1987. "Now, it has reunited us."

Family had always been the anchor in Ripken's life. It helped sculpt his demeanor, his drive, his destiny. His first year in the minors, he got major league homesick, telephoning his father as often to hear his gravelly voice as to ask for batting tips.

Earlier still, "Calvin" went AWOL in his first month of grade school, chugging away from Bakersfield Elementary School as fast as any Ripken's legs could go.

"He was a rascal, I'm telling you," said Olga Mapp Stansbury, who taught at the school. "When his parents dropped him off, he'd refuse to get out of the car. Then, as soon as we got ahold of him, they'd take off. If we didn't have a good, firm hold, he'd run."

Where?

"Home," Ripken said. "That was my intent. I knew how to get there, and it wasn't that far."

Why?

"Separation anxiety," he said. "Our family was close, and it was traumatic for me to be away from them."

Home was where his heart was. Also his bat and ball.

How quickly did Ripken warm to the game?

"How soon could he walk and drag a Wiffle bat behind him?" asked his mother, Vi.

One Christmas, Ripken found a wooden bat beneath the tree and began imitating his father's stroke— in the dining room. With the family china in jeopardy, Vi exchanged the ball for rolled-up socks.

Outdoors, Ripken could swing from the heels. In the hilly yard beside their split-level home on Clover Street, the Ripken brood– Cal, Bill, Fred and Elly– spent countless hours tussling, roughhousing. Competing. Balls dotted the yard like wild mushrooms.

Before his managerial assignment at Tri-City, Cal Ripken Sr. managed for two seasons at Aberdeen, S.D., where his wife Vi and sons Cal Jr. (left) and Fred cheered on the Class A Pheasants. (Bill wasn't born until December 1964.) Cal Sr. spent 14 years as a minor league manager— three of them at Aberdeen (1963, 1964 and 1966).

"We'd get up every day and play games," Fred remembered. "If you didn't feel good, tough, you still played. I never remember Cal getting sick or hurt and not playing. When he got old enough, a sprained ankle might have gotten him out of cutting the grass, but not out of playing ball."

The Ripken gang played hard. Small matter if a home run ball broke glass. Cal Sr. replaced many a garage window without a word.

"Dad only got mad if we broke windows from the inside out, which meant we were doing something we shouldn't have," Fred said.

The area was rural then, more cows than kids; the Ripkens had each other. They rode bicycles, skated and built forts in the trees across the road. On steamy summer afternoons, they escaped into those leafy woods, hewing paths with their sheath knives, cannonballing in an old swimming hole and fishing in a sleepy brook.

If they caught a wriggling catfish, they peeled it with pliers and cooked it on a makeshift grill from a refrigerator junked nearby.

Baseball basics, the kids got from their father. When he was home, Cal Sr. corralled them into the back yard to practice. He hit endless ground balls, which caromed off skinny arms, legs and chests.

Complaints were shrugged off. "The ball only weighs 5¼ ounces," the father would say. "How much can it hurt?"

Those early drills were "almost militaristic," Cal Jr. recalled. "Dad taught us how to to do something right, and then he'd expect us to do it that way every time." The Oriole Way.

By age 8, when Ripken joined Little League, those fundamentals were second nature.

"He needed no batting instruction," said Hank Paulick, his coach on the Angels in the Aberdeen Rec League. "Back then (1969), many kids went into a Pete Rose crouch and unwound like a rubber band. Cal's was a classic stand-up stance. When he swung, he'd swivel on the ball of his right foot and the heel of his left.

Cal was a terror hitting a Wiffle ball, riding a bike and displaying his baseball form to sister Elly.

"Boy, he had that swing down pat."

His first year in rec ball, Ripken batted .923; half of his hits went for extra bases.

"Cal was one of our best hitters, real intense," said Paulick. "His mother used

to drive him to practice and before the car stopped–it was still rolling, honest—he'd be out that door and running toward the field."

Watching him play, from her beat-up yellow-and-white lawn chair, Vi Ripken was struck by the depth of Cal's involvement.

"While other kids on the bench elbowed each other and horsed around," she said, "Junior sat at the end, watching the pitcher, waiting to hit, absorbed in the game."

The Ripkens were weaned on such attentiveness.

"Cal's work ethic, he got from Dad," Bill Ripken said.

All of the kids learned to spell from studying the sports pages—a mixed blessing. You weren't a Ripken if you couldn't read box scores.

Cal Sr. rarely made his sons' games. But he did bring home neat stuff from work: an aged batting cage here, a wheezy old pitching machine there.

Cal Jr. spent untold hours in the back yard, honing his swing on the 80-mph lobs of that mechanical arm until dusk, or until he'd driven all the balls into the woods across the road.

All the while, the 10-year-old imagined himself a pro—not an Orioles slugger like Boog Powell or Frank Robinson, but Class AA farmhands like Don Hickey and Terry Clapp, who had played for Cal's dad.

Every summer, the family set off for the boonies to find Pop. Vi packed the old Mercury, loaded up the kids and Scoobie, the dog, and motored off to Asheville, N.C., or Aberdeen, S.D., or Kennewick, Wash. (the Tri-City franchise)—wherever Cal Sr. happened to be preaching The Oriole Word.

Whatever the burg, the ballpark played baby-sitter. From an early age, the

At age 8, Cal (center, back row) played for the Angels Rec League team in his hometown of Aberdeen, Md., located 30 miles northeast of Baltimore. He already had his swing down pat, says his coach, who remembers the young Ripken as "real intense."

His first year in rec ball, Ripken batted .923; half of his hits went for extra bases.

The Family

children took in all of their father's home games (Elly made her stadium debut at 6 weeks). Sometimes they played games of their own behind the stands: The ball was a crumpled soda cup; the bat a rolled-up scorecard. The bases were napkins, ketchup-side down to adhere to the ground.

Cal rarely took his eyes off the field. Night after night, he sat in the stands, immersed in play. When his siblings were old enough, they began working the games, selling hot dogs and sweeping the clubhouse. Cal was to be batboy, only he balked at the job.

"All I wanted to do was sit and watch the games," he said. "I was a 'why' kid. I was fascinated by when things were done and why."

Game over, he hurried to the clubhouse and tagged along beside his dad, soaking in the sounds, smells and strategies. Players mussed his hair and dubbed him "Little Rip."

Later, when everyone else had dressed and gone and the ballpark fell silent, Cal would slip into his father's office, readying a lineup of questions. Why did this batter drag a bunt? Why did that one hit and run? The manager would shove aside his paperwork, light another cigarette and answer every one.

This was, Cal Sr. reasoned, explaining the real facts of life.

"That was my private time with him," Cal Jr. said. "I cherished those moments alone with my dad."

Every word sank in.

"Look at our environment back then," he said. "Baseball was beating on our heads every day. The normal conversation at dinner was baseball. We had access to all the players. Think of all those boring baseball clinics, in school gymnasiums, where all you do is sit on some wooden seat and listen.

"I had real-life clinics all the time. I had people to answer my questions."

At age 11, Ripken was promoted from the bleachers to the ball field. In Asheville, N.C., in 1972, he made road trips with the club, sat on the bench and wore the team uniform.

"I remember the way Cal put on that uniform—exactly as his dad did it," said Doug DeCinces, who played for the Orioles' Class AA team that season. "When I put on my socks differently, he looked at me and said, 'Why are you doing it that way?'

"Like, if it wasn't the way his dad did it, it must not be right."

Ripken sharpened his skills during batting practice in those bush-league parks, shagging flies off the wood of rising young Orioles stars like DeCinces, Al Bumbry and Bobby Grich. Players got a kick out of watching the Ripken kids tear across the outfield, arms outstretched, trying gamely but often missing balls by a couple of feet.

"When you did catch one, you were pretty proud of yourself," Cal said. Gradually, he began hobnobbing with players and picking up pointers. But he always bounced a tip off his father before putting it to practice.

"If Dad said that player was correct, I'd go back to that person and hang

When the Ripken kids engaged in a little high jinks in the sand, beachwear seemed in order—except, that is, for Cal, who was always ready to play a little ball.

When Cal was a freshman in high school, his father paid a visit to the baseball field. Aghast at the condition of the playing surface, Cal Sr. decided to give it a manicure.

The Family

around him some more," he said. "If Dad said he was wrong, I'd move along to the next one."

Being the manager's son meant sticking up for him in town. When someone hollered, "Your old man's a bum," the Ripkens closed ranks. Sometimes they took their lumps; more often, they dished them out.

"We almost got stoned off a school playground in Rochester (N.Y.) because some kids didn't like our dad," Fred said. "But we had the last laugh. We could throw stones farther than they could. We had better bloodlines."

The offseason brought all the Ripkens home, albeit for a few brief months. Even in winter, baseball took precedence. On weekends, Cal Sr. ferried his brood down the road to an abandoned school. There, in the deserted gym, he spent hours hitting them grounders on the hardwood floors. It was a test of fire; balls ricocheted off the ground at breakneck speeds. You either caught them or became a walking bruise.

Come spring, though, Cal Sr. was gone. You can count on one hand the times he saw his sons play in high school, and only then in hurried fragments. He did pop in before Cal's freshman season, to inspect the field at Aberdeen High. Rip studied the diamond, shook his head and stormed off in disgust. He returned with a homemade drag attached to the back of his old Chevrolet and swept the field, round and round, until it was "right."

Bill shrugged off his father's absence. "It wasn't like Pops said he would come, and then not show up," he said.

Cal was less tolerant: "I wanted to brag and say, 'My dad is here.' I wanted him to pat me on the back and say, 'Good job.'

In his senior year at Aberdeen High, Ripken (front row, center) batted a team-high .492 and struck out just four times. Three strikeouts came in the only complete game his father ever watched.

"He saw portions of five of my games. When he was there, I'd try to show off, and consequently not do as well. By the time the game was over, he'd be gone."

In his senior year at Aberdeen High, Ripken batted a team-high .492 and struck out just four times. Three strikeouts came in one day—the only complete game his father ever watched. He made an error "showing off" in that game, too, he said.

No matter. The Orioles drafted him.

For Ripken, 1987 began on a positive note. Forget the club's last-place finish of the year before. Baltimore had a new manager, its longtime third base coach whose name and steel-blue eyes matched those of his All-Star shortstop.

"It feels good to see my dad take charge," Ripken said.

Cal Sr. (above, with Cal Jr., and opposite, hitting grounders) managed the Orioles for one season and six games into another. Cal Jr. was diplomatic about his dismissal; Bill was less reserved.

Already, Cal was an established star. And now his brother, Bill, had a chance to make the club in spring training.

"I've dreamed about Billy and me playing side by side," Cal told reporters in Florida. "I'd be fibbing if I didn't say I was pulling for him–and to play together for our father would be great."

That spring, the Ripken brothers worked as one. They dressed two lockers apart, ran wind sprints together, wore the same-style dress shoes. Cal Sr. watched his offspring intently, outwardly unimpressed.

"This is good," was all he'd say.

Bill was optioned to Class AAA Rochester, but he was called up by Baltimore July 11 as the Orioles attempted to rebound from their horrid (31-50) start. Cal met him before the game, cooked Bill a steak and chauffeured him to Memorial Stadium.

The Orioles lost that night, but they won their next 11 games before faltering

New Orioles manager Cal Ripken Sr. and coach Elrod Hendricks chat during an intrasquad game in the spring of 1987. Baltimore got off to a poor regular-season start in '87 and had an even worse beginning in 1988.

again. They finished 67-95. Bill played well, hitting .308 for his dad. Cal finished at .252.

At his wedding that winter, Cal's best man was his manager; the ushers, his brothers. At the reception, Cal Sr. made a touching toast: "May the most that you desire be the least that you accomplish." In baseball, as in life.

Alas, the honeymoon was over. Six winless games into the 1988 season, Cal Sr. was fired. (The club would start the season 0-21, a big-league record for futility.)

Publicly, when asked to comment, Cal Jr. played the diplomat.

"I'm a player–I'm not supposed to have an opinion on that," he told the media. "As a son ... I'll keep my opinions to myself."

Bill was less reserved. He immediately switched jerseys, taking his father's No. 7 in protest.

"It didn't make me the happiest person in the world," he later said of his dad's firing.

Bill's average plummeted to .207 that season, a year in which he played a career-high 150 games. Cal hit .264.

That quickly, the Ripken "era" was over.

"We had high hopes for better things," Vi Ripken said years later. "It filled me with pride the first time to see three of my guys in the same uniform, and on the same field.

"That hasn't happened to many families. It was a moment to revel in—and to cherish."

The Family

Cal dreamed of playing alongside brother Bill (right)—and his dream came true. Better yet, the two wound up playing for their father.

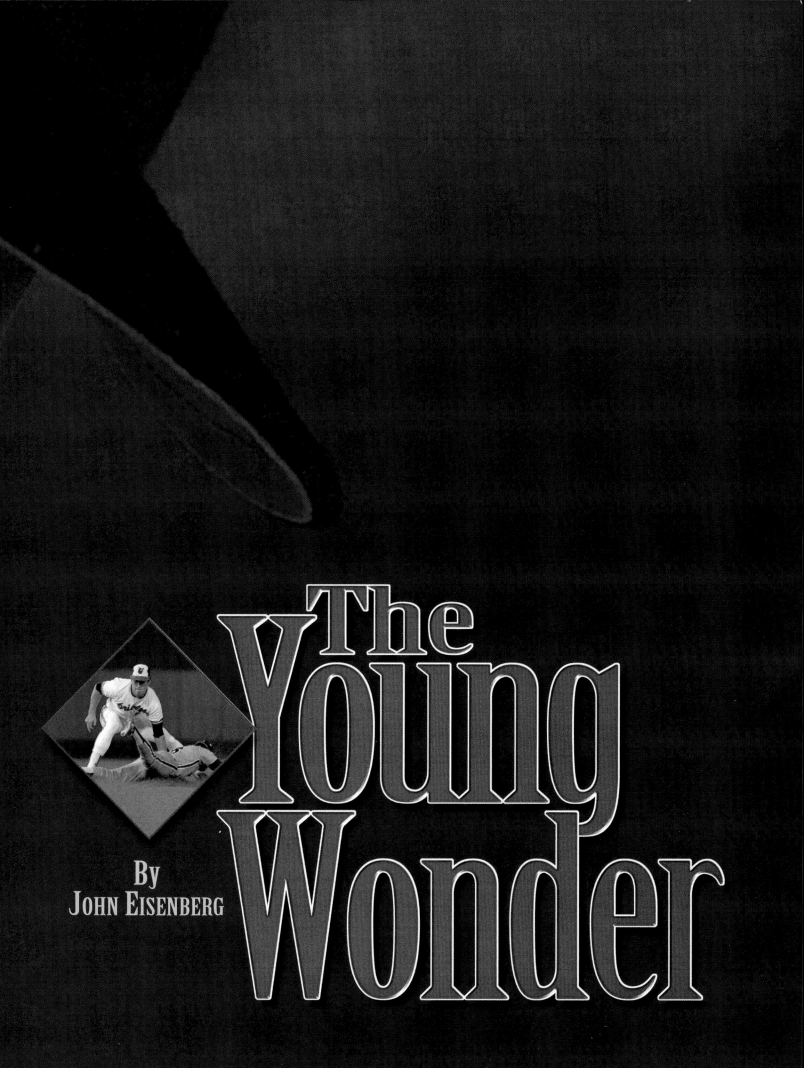

The Young Wonder

By
JOHN EISENBERG

The Young Wonder

Cal Ripken accomplished enough in the early years of his career to last a lifetime. His name would later become synonymous with more understated and industrious traits such as steadiness and dependability, but he was a shooting star in his first years with the Orioles, a supernova streaking across the American League skies. Before his 24th birthday, he had played on a World Series winner, won Rookie of the Year and Most Valuable Player honors in the American League and made the first of his many All-Star Game appearances. He also had played in 280 consecutive games by the end of the 1983 season, starting his pursuit of Lou Gehrig's record.

The big, blue-eyed kid with uncanny instincts and a third base coach for a father obviously was something special.

Such a beginning was hard to envision when the Orioles selected Ripken in the second round of the 1978 amateur draft, the 48th pick overall. The son of Cal Ripken Sr., a player, coach and instructor in the Orioles' system since 1957, he had pitched and played shortstop at Aberdeen (Md.) High School, winning seven of nine decisions with a 0.70 ERA as a senior while hitting .492 with 29 RBIs in 20 games. Those were impressive numbers, and Orioles scout Dick Bowie had recommended him highly, but he was just the club's fourth overall selection on draft day.

"They never would have drafted him if it hadn't been for his father," said former Orioles general manager Frank Cashen. "There was a report circulating from a free-lance, veteran scout, and it was all about his pitching, saying he was going to have to be a pitcher as a professional. The report said that he could hit, but that his body was too heavy for him to play anywhere else, so he would have to pitch."

Before turning 24, Ripken had won Rookie of the Year and MVP honors in the American League and played on a World Series champion.

The Young Wonder

Ripken said: "I was scouted very heavily as a pitcher. As a matter of fact, I think the Orioles were the only team looking at me and thinking of me as anything other than a pitcher."

The Orioles held several rounds of internal discussions after the draft, trying to decide what to do with Ripken. "There was a split in the organization, some saying pitcher and some saying shortstop," Ripken said.

"Dick Bowie wanted me to be a regular player. (Orioles manager) Earl Weaver wanted me to hit. Some others wanted me to pitch. Ultimately, the choice was presented to me, and I said, 'I want to play every day.'"

After enduring an error-prone season playing shortstop for the Orioles' rookie-league affiliate in Bluefield, W.Va., he began to emerge as an organizational jewel. He hit .303 for Class A Miami in 1979, then had 25 homers and 78 RBIs for Class AA Charlotte in 1980 and was named a Southern League All-Star. Along the way, he had been moved to third base, with the organization viewing the more polished, accomplished Bob Bonner as the heir apparent to longtime Orioles shortstop Mark Belanger, who was nearing retirement.

After playing on a title-winning team in Puerto Rican winter ball, Ripken made his first appearance at the Orioles' spring training camp in Miami in 1981.

"Just the sight of him that spring was shocking," said Mike Flanagan, a veteran Orioles pitcher that year. "We'd last seen him as a high school kid with his dad throwing him batting practice, and in those days you looked at his (slightly built) dad and figured he wasn't going to get much bigger. But then he showed up that spring and he was this big, young guy with a lot of power, and

Ripken's first major
league home run—off
the Royals' Dennis
Leonard—came on
opening day in 1982.
As Cal rounded third,
there was a familiar
face to greet him.

you said to yourself, 'My gosh, how much bigger is he going to get?' "

Ripken opened the 1981 season as the third baseman for Class AAA
Rochester, one step away from the major leagues. On opening day, Rochester
manager Doc Edwards pinch hit for him with the game on the line in the ninth
inning, sending Tom Chism to the plate. Chism singled in the winning run, but
Ripken made certain Edwards never considered replacing him again. He hit 14
home runs early in the season, and never slowed down. When a 50-day strike
halted the major league season, a crew from *This Week in Baseball* toured the
minors interviewing the game's coming stars, and Ripken was among those
profiled. "I knew I was on the verge of getting called up," Ripken said.

The call came on August 8, 1981, just after the strike was settled. Ripken
made his major league debut as a pinch runner in a win over the Royals on
August 10 in Baltimore. His first hit came six days later, a single off Chicago
pitcher Dennis Lamp at Memorial Stadium. But with Doug DeCinces entrenched
as the Orioles' third baseman and the club contending for a playoff berth, Ripken
mostly just watched instead of played. His total offensive production for his
seven weeks in Baltimore consisted of five singles and a walk. "To me, it seemed

The Young Wonder

like I got the at-bats DeCinces didn't want," Ripken said.

Despite that unimpressive debut, Ripken was at the heart of an intense organizational debate after the season. He had batted .288 with 23 homers and 75 RBIs in 114 games at Rochester. Was he ready to play every day in the major leagues? If so, where? Third base? Shortstop? Weaver wanted him to take over at shortstop, now that Belanger had moved on to the Dodgers for his final big-league season, but Orioles G.M. Hank Peters had groomed Bonner as Belanger's replacement and envisioned Ripken at third. But what about DeCinces, a solid veteran who hit with power and played well in the field?

The debate was settled in shocking fashion—DeCinces was traded to the Angels in January 1982, sealing Ripken's ascendancy to the starting lineup as a third baseman. DeCinces said years later that he felt he was traded because of his union activities—he was the Orioles' player representative during the strike—but Peters denied the charge. "The only factors that entered into making the trade were that Doug had a major back problem and we needed to make room for Cal," Peters said.

Ripken opened the 1982 season as the Orioles' third baseman and hit a home

Whether camping under a popup or swinging a productive bat, Ripken was a take-charge guy in his rookie season.

run in his first at-bat on opening day at Memorial Stadium. "Ken Singleton was on base ahead of me, and I chased him around the bases with my heart going 3,000 mph," Ripken recalled. But after going 3-for-5 in the opener, he fell into a horrific slump, managing just four hits in his next 55 at-bats. Fastballs sailed by him as he waited for breaking balls. He was batting .117 on May 1.

"Earl called me into the office a few times," Ripken said. "I think he was trying to play some mind games with me, saying, 'Look, we don't have anybody else. We traded DeCinces, so you're not going anywhere. I'm not sending you down. We don't have anybody else. You're it. All right. See you later.' And just kicked me out of the office."

Ripken finally got going with some help from, of all people, rival slugger Reggie Jackson of the Angels, who gave him a pep talk one night while standing

on third base. Ripken scratched out a couple of infield hits, began to feel comfortable and started producing. Batting sixth in the order, he became a steady contributor as the Orioles chased front-running Milwaukee in the A.L. East.

Then there was the position change orchestrated by Weaver, who trumped Peters and moved Ripken to shortstop on July 1. The move was made after Bonner crumbled under Weaver's withering stare early in the season, playing some shaky defense, failing to hit and ultimately getting sent back to the minors. Bonner's stunning collapse left the club without a future at shortstop, and Weaver moved Ripken into the breach.

Ripken (center) says Eddie Murray, with whom he shared a passion for playing the game right, offered advice and comfort when he struggled early in 1982. Murray was in his sixth year in the majors; Cal was in his first full year after a 23-game stint in '81.

"I came in that night and happened to glance at the lineup and noticed the 6 next to my name, where I was used to seeing the 5," Ripken said. "I thought, 'Well, sometimes you make mistakes when you write out the lineup.' I sat down at my locker and started getting dressed, and (teammate) Lenn Sakata came over to me and said, 'You know, you're playing short tonight.' And I said, 'Well, I saw that 6 by my name, but I haven't played shortstop in a long time. I can't be playing shortstop, there's got to be a mistake.' And he goes, 'No, it's not a mistake.'

"I went to my dad—his locker was right across the way—and I said, 'Am I playing short?' And he goes, 'Yeah.' He kind of talked to me. This was just totally out of the blue, no warning. I didn't take ground balls or anything ahead of time. It was just, 'You're playing short today.' So then Earl called me into the office and said, 'Look, I'm putting you at short. Trying to get some more offense in the lineup. I don't want you to do too much. If the ball's hit to you, just catch it, take it out (of the glove), get a good grip on the ball, make sure you're balanced, take your time and make a good throw to first base. OK? That's all I want you to do.' That was his version of a pep talk. I thought it was still temporary, that I was ultimately going back to third. But I didn't go back for 15 years."

Weaver said: "I had grown up in St Louis watching Marty Marion, a 6-2 shortstop with the Cardinals, and he just seemed to take two steps and reach out and have the ball in his glove. And there was no question about Rip's arm at that

The Young Wonder

The Young Wonder

time. He had a great arm."

Ripken struggled at first, but he grew more comfortable as the season went on, and his hitting flourished, too. He ended up leading all major league rookies in home runs (28), RBIs (93), doubles (32) and runs (90), and although the Orioles lost to the Brewers on the last day of the season to miss the playoffs, Ripken was named the A.L.'s Rookie of the Year, beating out Minnesota's Kent Hrbek and Boston's Wade Boggs.

"He was just different than most rookies," Singleton said. "You could see that he was well-schooled. He knew exactly where he was supposed to play in the field. And he was a good enough hitter already. He batted down in the lineup and had some solid numbers. And his personality was just like his dad's: all business. 'We're going to win if we do it right.' I can't say that we had the sense at that time that he was going to become this mega-mega-star. But we knew he was going to be a star player."

It was during his rookie season that Ripken became friendly with Eddie Murray, Baltimore's star first baseman. Murray, a six-year veteran in 1982, had been schooled by Ripken's father in the Orioles' system, and he helped indoctrinate the younger Ripken to the majors, on and off the field. In return, the playful Ripken helped loosen up the tightly wound Murray. Recognizing a shared passion for playing the game right, they became soulmates and best friends.

"The year before in Rochester (in 1981) was the first time I'd had an apartment by myself, but it seemed like I wasn't connected to the real nucleus of that team, because everybody was so much older," Ripken said. "And then you come to the big leagues, and it was worse than that. Everybody else was older and had families. Eddie and I were single. When we came back from road trips, the families and wives were at the airport picking them up, and Eddie and I were catching the bus to satellite parking and picking up our cars. We started hanging out together and became really exceptional friends. When I was struggling, he offered me advice and comfort and tried to include me. I was very grateful."

Ripken felt established and ready to excel as the Orioles convened in Miami for spring training in 1983. They were a veteran club that had won a pennant in 1979 and come close to making the playoffs every season since, yet always come up just short. Now Weaver was gone, retired to the golf course in Florida. The new manager was low-key Joe Altobelli.

"The smartest thing Joe did was come in and not change a thing," Ripken said. "That was a good, veteran team that ran itself, and he came in and guided it. We had watched the Brewers celebrate on the field after the last game (the year before), and we were very motivated."

The Orioles lost on opening day, endured a seven-game losing streak in May and were just four games over .500 at the beginning of June, with injuries to Flanagan and Jim Palmer disturbing the starting rotation.

But after another seven-game losing streak dropped them to fourth in early August, the Orioles got hot and took charge of the division. No one was hotter than Ripken, who batted .391 as the Orioles won 34 of 44 games in an August-September stretch to lock up the A.L. East title. In Minnesota, he had a five-hit game, including two homers and two doubles.

"He was just different than most rookies. You could see that he was well-schooled. He knew exactly where he was supposed to play in the field. ... And his personality was just like his dad's: all business."

—Ken Singleton, former teammate

Ripken played a key
role in Baltimore's
1983 ALCS triumph
over the White Sox,
batting .400 and
scoring five runs.

At age 23, in his second full season in the majors, the traits that would mark him as a player throughout his career were now in bloom. He didn't have exceptional range at shortstop, but he always seemed to be in the right place at the right time, utilizing his grasp of pitchers' tendencies, hitters' habits, the count, the weather conditions and the playing surface.

"He was replacing Belanger, who was so intelligent, but he was just as intelligent and calculating," Flanagan said. "And we had such good pitching in those days that he could count on the pitcher locating the pitch exactly, which meant the ball would go where he thought it should go. He was really good in those days at cheating a couple of steps in one direction and getting to balls, because he knew the pitch would be good."

At the plate, batting third in the order with Murray behind him, he was a force. As in the field, he was a thinking man's hitter more than a natural, already expert at the guessing game with the pitcher that unfolded on every at-bat. "I like to figure out situations," he told a reporter late in the season. "I think about what the pitcher has that day and what he might throw me."

Playing every inning of every game, he led the major leagues in hits (211) and

The Young Wonder

doubles (47). He also led the A.L. in runs scored (121) and extra-base hits (76), and he batted .318. "He's been amazing," Singleton told a reporter as the playoffs began. "I think we expected him to raise his average a little bit in his second season, but he's really come on."

He batted .400 and scored five runs as the Orioles eliminated the Chicago White Sox in four games in the American League Championship Series, sending Baltimore into the World Series against a veteran Philadelphia Phillies team that included Mike Schmidt, Pete Rose, Joe Morgan, Tony Perez and Steve Carlton.

"I still remember going to the World Series, the way it was covered, the different atmosphere, all the media on the field, the level of importance, the enormity of it, what you're playing for," Ripken said. "I was scared, and it took me getting one ground ball to calm down. You got the ball and threw it, and somewhere it just clicked, saying, 'Well, that's what I've been doing all year. That's baseball.' There was that point when you got over it, and then everything was fine."

The Phillies won the Series opener at Memorial Stadium, but the Orioles evened things in the next game with Ripken singling in a key run in the seventh inning of a 4-1 win. The Orioles then went to Philadelphia and swept three games to bring home their first World Series title in 13 years. Ripken hit just .167 in the five games, but he made the last putout of the Series, catching Gary Maddox's soft line drive, and he began leaping with joy, symbolizing the Orioles' triumph.

In the clubhouse celebration, Altobelli approached Ripken with champagne

Playing in his first World Series in '83 at age 23, Ripken was struck by the enormity of the event.

After the Orioles dispatched the Phils in five games in the '83 World Series, Ripken and teammate Dan Ford bubbled over with enthusiasm.

dripping off his cap. "I'm not going to let that happen again next year," the manager said. "I'm not going to play you every game."

It was a promise he didn't keep.

The ultimate team success was matched by the ultimate individual honor several weeks later, when Ripken was named the A.L.'s Most Valuable Player by the Baseball Writers' Association of America. He narrowly beat out Murray, his teammate and best friend, finishing with 322 points to 290 for Murray. There was some controversy, as Murray had finished the season with six more homers and nine more RBIs than Ripken, but Ripken had a higher average (Murray batted .306), 33 more hits, 17 more doubles and six more runs scored.

"I knew one of the two was going to win," Singleton said. "I knew the guy who didn't win was going to finish second. Personally, I thought Eddie had been around longer and should have won, simply because there should be a pecking order. Cal was the new kid on the block. But he was terrific and equally deserving, and it didn't bother me that he won because they both had carried the team all season."

The veteran Orioles certainly wouldn't have gone all the way without the injection of Ripken's youthful brilliance. "He brought them the World Series title in 1983, there's no doubt about it," Weaver said years later. "Rookie of the Year one year, American League MVP the next. That's some way to start a career."

Not even 24 yet, and already one of the game's brightest lights.

Fans mobbed Ripken and the rest of the 1983 World Series champion Orioles in a victory parade in the streets of downtown Baltimore.

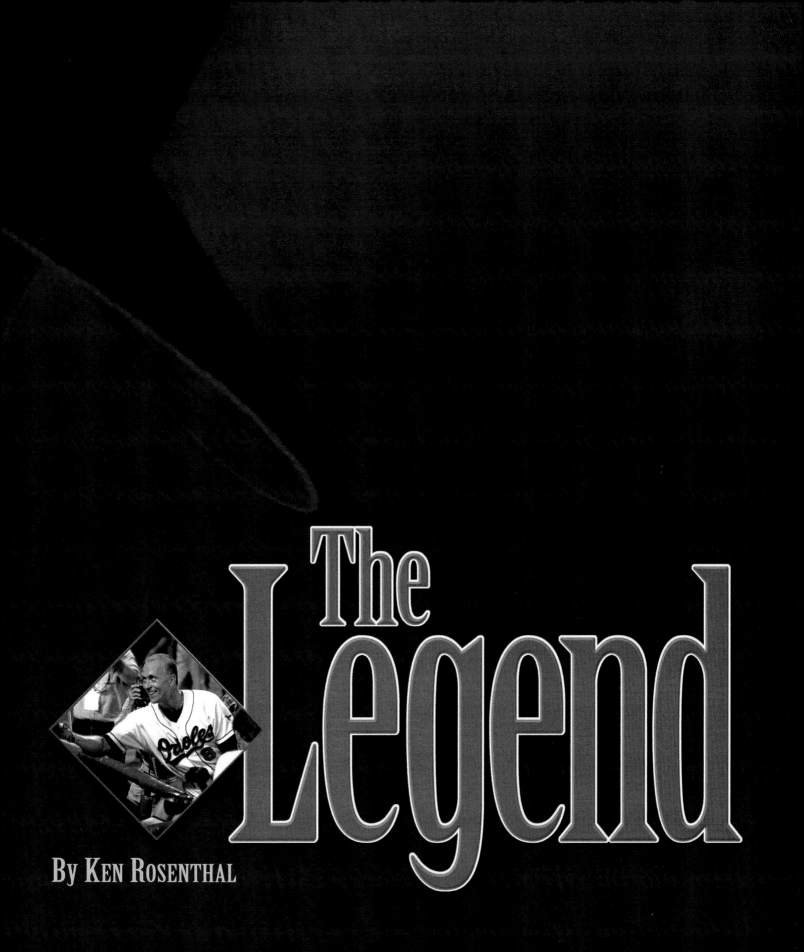

The Legend

By Ken Rosenthal

The Legend

His nickname, "The Iron Man," was a logical extension of Lou Gehrig's nickname, "The Iron Horse." It revealed nothing about the immense baseball skill of Cal Ripken Jr. But it was the perfect description of a player whose appearance in a record 2,632 consecutive games transformed him into something more than a perennial All-Star.

The Streak is Ripken's baseball legacy, dwarfing everything else he accomplished in 21 years with the Orioles, reducing his career statistics to mere numbers on a baseball card. Gehrig's plaque at Yankee Stadium's Monument Park says his "record of 2,130 consecutive games should stand for all time." Those words proved an exaggeration, but it's safe to assume that no one will come close to playing as many consecutive games as Ripken did. No one will even try.

Ripken's greater legacy, however, goes beyond his sport. Few professional athletes commanded as much respect during the period in which he played, from 1981 to 2001. He wasn't as accomplished in baseball as Michael Jordan was in basketball or Wayne Gretzky was in hockey, but he held similar stature. The Streak was a singular, breathtaking achievement, and the night that Ripken broke Lou Gehrig's record—September 6, 1995—will forever be etched in the memory of the American sporting public.

To an extent, Ripken was in the right place at the right time, playing in a media age that created new levels of stardom. But the increased media brought increased scrutiny, and Ripken rarely, if ever, took a public misstep. His grace and humility earned him universal admiration from fans. His commitment and professionalism earned him the lasting admiration of his peers.

Who will carry his mantle? No active major leaguer shares Ripken's knack for always playing the

The Streak is Cal Ripken Jr.'s baseball legacy, as he and his fans (opposite page) proved on the memorable night of September 6, 1995.

The Legend

game correctly, always making the proper choices, always saying the right things. Not Mark McGwire, who often comes off as petulant in interviews. Not Alex Rodriguez, who modeled himself after Ripken but turned off many fans by signing a $252 million contract. Derek Jeter's squeaky-clean image probably is the closest to Ripken's, but can he sustain it for 10 more years playing for the Yankees? Doubtful.

Longevity always was a goal of Ripken's, and he met his goal of spending his entire career with one club, following the example of his childhood hero, Orioles Hall of Fame third baseman Brooks Robinson. Fifteen players overall, including fellow retiree Tony Gwynn, have spent 20 or more seasons with the same team. More could follow, though the feat is becoming increasingly difficult to accomplish in the free-agent era. Jeter will be a 15-year veteran with the Yankees when his latest contract expires. At that point, he'll be 36, a millionaire 200 times over. He might not want to play five more years.

Professional athletes frequently stumble all over themselves, complaining

The Legend

about their contracts, leading questionable personal lives, falling victim to drugs or alcohol. Ripken almost never took a misstep, not when the Orioles fired his late father, Cal Ripken Sr. as manager, not when critics called for him to end The Streak, not when his hometown Orioles disintegrated in both the late 1980s and '90s. He led a careful, calculating existence, but it served him well. In an age of endless self-promotion, he maintained a sensible, humble demeanor. Fans loved him for it. He shut up and played.

He was a great player, too, but Ripken probably won't be remembered as the best power-hitting shortstop—Alex Rodriguez, who grew up in Miami with a poster of Ripken on his wall, figures to surpass him. Ripken almost certainly won't be remembered as the best defensive shortstop, either—Omar Vizquel and Ozzie Smith were more spectacular players at the position. But McGwire is the only player of recent times who came close to elevating baseball in a similar manner, and he had Sammy Sosa to help shoulder the burden during his record 70-homer season in 1998. McGwire later admitted that Ripken created the blueprint for how to handle increased fan and media attention during his countdown to Gehrig's record.

Without The Streak, Ripken's place in history probably would be similar to that of Red Sox Hall of Fame outfielder Carl Yastrzemski. Like Yaz, Ripken spent his entire career with one team. Like Yaz, Ripken is one of seven members of the 400-homer, 3,000-hit club. Yaz won seven Gold Gloves to Ripken's two, but Ripken won two Most Valuable Player awards to Yaz's one. The difference between the two? Yaz's defining accomplishment—his 1967 Triple Crown—was purely a baseball accomplishment. The Streak took Ripken to another level. Even

After Ripken played in consecutive-game No. 2,131, Baltimore fans lined the streets to pay homage to the game's new Iron Man.

non-sports fans could admire a player who showed up every day for work, beginning in 1982 and ending in 1998. Ripken was one of them. He just happened to play baseball.

◆ ◆ ◆

Ripken wasn't as accomplished a hitter as Gwynn (eight National League batting titles, 17 consecutive seasons, 50 or more games, of batting .300) and he wasn't any better a role model. Gwynn, too, was a tremendous student of the game, one of the sport's true gentlemen, a player who spent two decades with the same team. But Ripken was more revered around the country, and he left the sport to greater fanfare.

Location had something to do with Gwynn receiving less adulation—he played in San Diego, on the opposite side of the country from the East Coast media centers (Baltimore's proximity to Washington, D.C., enabled both president Bill Clinton and vice president Albert Gore to witness Ripken's breaking of Gehrig's record at Camden Yards). Gwynn also chose to maintain a lower profile, remaining with his hometown Padres in part because he wanted less media attention.

Another difference was in the history that each man chased. Ripken engaged in a daily, methodical pursuit of a supposedly unbreakable record belonging to Gehrig, one of the most tragic figures in sports history. Gwynn's record pursuits—most batting titles, most consecutive seasons batting .300—were more obscure. The player who holds those marks, Ty Cobb, was, by all accounts, a

wretched person. And, of course, Gwynn fell six consecutive .300 seasons and four batting titles short.

The final difference was that Ripken remained productive until the end of his career, while injuries limited Gwynn to 102 at-bats in his last season. Ripken delighted fans on several of his farewell stops by hitting home runs after emotional pregame retirement ceremonies. He also hit a home run and was named MVP of his final All-Star Game at Seattle's Safeco Field while Gwynn watched from the National League dugout, sidelined by an injured hamstring.

Gwynn appeared in two World Series, Ripken one. If Ripken had one regret, it's that he often was the entire show in Baltimore, drawing attention with his various milestone pursuits as the Orioles limped to another losing season. Ripken had a flair for the dramatic, but his teams rarely were good enough to benefit. Unlike Michael Jordan (six NBA titles) and Wayne Gretzky (four Stanley Cups), Ripken won only one World Series championship, in his second full season with the Orioles. Though he never intended to set himself apart. The Streak enabled him to transcend his team, and even his sport.

◆ ◆ ◆

Imagine if Ripken had devoted all of his considerable energy to a profession other than baseball. If he had been a politician, he would have been a tireless campaigner. If he had been an author, he would have been uncommonly prolific.

Ripken was always accessible to young fans despite his star billing, which rose again in 2001 when he was named All-Star Game MVP (opposite page).

The Legend

If he had been a doctor, he would have worked around the clock in emergency rooms, tending to one patient after another.

Well, for the first time since '82, Ripken no longer is a major league baseball player. It is doubtful he will ever leave the sport; his first post-retirement initiative will be the completion of the Aberdeen Project, a state-of-the-art youth baseball academy in his hometown of Aberdeen, Md. But Ripken, 41, is still a relatively young man. Who knows what he might achieve?

A superstar with a near-perfect image is a superstar with power, but Ripken rarely chose to exert his influence as a player. Even though he is deeply opinionated, he steered clear of controversial topics, remaining above the fray during the Orioles' most turbulent periods. Like Jordan, he occasionally received media criticism for his reluctance to take a stand—Ripken's words on any number of issues would have spoken volumes. His image, however, remained pristine.

It's doubtful that Ripken will change his public persona now that he is retired. His first priority is to spend more time with his children—Rachel, 11, and Ryan, 8. Maybe he will be content to devote the rest of his professional life to promoting youth baseball, a calling that would enable him to spread his love for the game and honor the memory of his father, the late Cal Sr.

Ripken plans an active role with the Cal Ripken Baseball Division of the Babe Ruth League for players 12-and-under. He's also contributing $11 million

Ripken is stepping to the plate as a key player in the Aberdeen Project, a youth baseball academy for which groundbreaking was held in late 2000.

The Legend

of the $25 million required for the Aberdeen Project. The complex will include a 6,500-seat minor league ballpark, housing for 400 players and coaches and six youth fields modeled after Yankee Stadium, Fenway Park, Ebbets Field, Wrigley Field and Baltimore's Memorial Stadium and Camden Yards. Ripken is involved in every detail, right down to writing instructional manuals.

"He seems to see things differently and larger than most people," says Ripken's younger brother, Bill, a former major leaguer who is working closely with Cal on the Aberdeen Project. "Somebody asked my Mom what would Dad think of this whole thing. Her quote was like, 'Damn, this is big.'

"As a teacher, nobody was better than Pops (Cal Ripken Sr.). But this is kind of beyond his scope of things. Junior seems to take it to the next level, sensing how big

One of Ripken's special traits—his flair for the dramatic—was evident in his final All-Star Game appearance when he hit a home run (opposite page).

The Legend

it can be. I never would have thrown this stuff out there if I was doing it myself."

But what happens once the project is up and running? Or further down the line, once Ripken's children are grown? As a player, Ripken was as legendary a competitor as Jordan. And he has spoken of his desire to "shape an organization" from a position similar to the one Jordan held as part owner and president of basketball operations for the Washington Wizards.

The Orioles are the most natural association for Ripken, the only organization that he has ever known. But the team's present owner, Peter Angelos, has had a series of problems with strong, independent-minded executives. Despite enviable resources, the Orioles have endured four consecutive losing seasons for the first time in their 48-year history. Ripken might not consider a position until Angelos sells the club.

Ripken also has been mentioned as a candidate to run a franchise in northern Virginia if a team relocates to that area, and he likely would be a popular choice for other teams as well. His baseball know-how is exceptional, and it's easy to imagine him evaluating talent, hiring top instructors, implementing the theories he learned from his father. He would need help on the administrative and management ends, but he certainly would understand how to work within the framework of a team.

Ripken will take all of the qualities that made him a great baseball player into his next career. A man with the will to play 2,632 consecutive games will be a force to be reckoned with—whatever path he chooses.

CAL RIPKEN

PERSONAL: Born August 24, 1960, in Havre de Grace, Md. ... 6-4/220. ... Bats right, throws right. ... Full name: Calvin Edwin Ripken Jr. ... Son of Cal Ripken Sr., minor league catcher (1957-62 and 1964), manager with Baltimore Orioles (1987-88) and coach, Orioles (1976-86 and 1989-92); and brother of Bill Ripken, infielder with four major league teams (1987-98).

HIGH SCHOOL: Aberdeen (Md.).

TRANSACTIONS/CAREER NOTES: Selected by Baltimore Orioles organization in second round of free-agent draft (June 6, 1978). ... On disabled list (April 18-May 13 and August 1-September 1, 1999, and June 28-September 1, 2000).

RECORDS: Holds major league career records for most consecutive games played—2,632 (May 30, 1982-September 19, 1998); most years leading league in games played—9; most consecutive years played all club's games—15 (1983-97); most years played all club's games—15 (1983-97); most home runs by shortstop—345; most years leading league in games by shortstop—12; most consecutive games by shortstop—2,216; and most years leading league in double plays by shortstop—8. ... Holds major league single-season records for most at-bats without a triple—646 (1989); highest fielding percentage by shortstop (150 or more games)—.996 (1990); fewest errors by shortstop (150 or more games)—3 (1990). ... Holds A.L. career records for most double plays by shortstop—1,565; most years leading league in putouts by shortstop—6; most consecutive years played 150 or more games—12 (1982-93); most years with 150 or more games played—15 (1982-93 and 1996-98). ... Holds A.L. single-season record for most assists by shortstop—583 (1984). ... Shares A.L. career record for most years leading league in assists by shortstop—7. ... Shares A.L. single-season record for most consecutive errorless games by shortstop—95 (April 14-July 27, 1990).

HONORS: Named A.L. Rookie Player of the Year by THE SPORTING NEWS (1982). ... Named A.L. Rookie of the Year by Baseball Writers' Association of America (1982). ... Named Major League Player of the Year by THE SPORTING NEWS (1983 and 1991). ... Named A.L. Player of the Year by THE SPORTING NEWS (1983 and 1991). ... Named shortstop on THE SPORTING NEWS A.L. All-Star team (1983-85, 1989, 1991 and 1993-95). ... Named shortstop on THE SPORTING NEWS A.L. Silver Slugger team (1983-86, 1989, 1991 and 1993-94). ... Named A.L. Most Valuable Player by Baseball Writers' Association of America (1983 and 1991). ... Won A.L. Gold Glove at shortstop (1991-92). ... Named Sportsman of the Year by THE SPORTING NEWS (1995).

STATISTICAL NOTES: Tied for Appalachian League lead with 329 total chances by shortstops and in double plays by shortstop with 31 in 1978. ... Led Southern League third basemen with .933 fielding percentage, 119 putouts, 268 assists, 415 total chances and 34 double plays in 1980. ... Tied for Southern League lead with nine sacrifice flies in 1980. ... Led A.L. shortstops with 831 total chances in 1983, 906 in 1984, 815 in 1989, 806 in 1991 and 738 in 1993. ... Led A.L. shortstops with 113 double plays in 1983, 122 in 1984, 123 in 1985, 119 in 1989, 114 in 1991, 72 in 1992, 72 in 1994 and 100 in 1995. ... Hit for the cycle (May 6, 1984). ... Tied for A.L. lead with 15 game-winning RBIs in 1986. ... Tied for A.L. lead with 10 sacrifice flies in 1988. ... Led A.L. with 368 total bases in 1991. ... Hit three home runs in one game (May 28, 1996). ... Led A.L. in grounding into double plays with 28 in 1996. ... Collected six hits in one game (June 13, 1999). ... Career major league grand slams: 8.

MISCELLANEOUS: Holds Baltimore Orioles all-time records for most hits (3,184), runs (1,647), doubles (603), home runs (431) and runs batted in (1,695).

| | | | | | | | — BATTING — | | | | | | | | — FIELDING — | | |
Year Team (League)	Pos.	G	AB	R	H	2B	3B	HR	RBI	Avg.	BB	SO	SB	PO	A	E	Avg.
1978—Bluefield (Appl.)	SS	63	239	27	63	7	1	0	24	.264	24	46	1	*92	204	*33	.900
1979—Miami (FSL)	3B-SS-2B	105	393	51	119	*28	1	5	54	.303	31	64	4	149	260	30	.932
—Charlotte (Sou.)	3B	17	61	6	11	0	1	3	8	.180	3	13	1	13	26	3	.929
1980—Charlotte (Sou.)	3B-SS	•144	522	91	144	28	5	25	78	.276	77	81	4	†151	†341	35	†.934
1981—Rochester (I.L.)	3B-SS	114	437	74	126	31	4	23	75	.288	66	85	0	128	320	21	.955
—Baltimore (A.L.)	SS-3B	23	39	1	5	0	0	0	0	.128	1	8	0	13	30	3	.935
1982—Baltimore (A.L.)	SS-3B	160	598	90	158	32	5	28	93	.264	46	95	3	221	440	19	.972
1983—Baltimore (A.L.)	SS	•162	*663	*121	*211	*47	2	27	102	.318	58	97	0	272	*534	25	.970
1984—Baltimore (A.L.)	SS	•162	641	103	195	37	7	27	86	.304	71	89	2	*297	*583	26	.971
1985—Baltimore (A.L.)	SS	161	642	116	181	32	5	26	110	.282	67	68	2	*286	474	26	.967
1986—Baltimore (A.L.)	SS	162	627	98	177	35	1	25	81	.282	70	60	4	240	*482	13	.982
1987—Baltimore (A.L.)	SS	*162	624	97	157	28	3	27	98	.252	81	77	3	240	*480	20	.973
1988—Baltimore (A.L.)	SS	161	575	87	152	25	1	23	81	.264	102	69	2	*284	480	21	.973
1989—Baltimore (A.L.)	SS	•162	646	80	166	30	0	21	93	.257	57	72	3	*276	*531	8	.990
1990—Baltimore (A.L.)	SS	161	600	78	150	28	4	21	84	.250	82	66	3	242	435	3	*.996
1991—Baltimore (A.L.)	SS	•162	650	99	210	46	5	34	114	.323	53	46	6	*267	*528	11	.986
1992—Baltimore (A.L.)	SS	*162	637	73	160	29	1	14	72	.251	64	50	4	*287	445	12	.984
1993—Baltimore (A.L.)	SS	*162	*641	87	165	26	3	24	90	.257	65	58	1	226	*495	17	.977
1994—Baltimore (A.L.)	SS	112	444	71	140	19	3	13	75	.315	32	41	1	132	321	7	*.985
1995—Baltimore (A.L.)	SS	144	550	71	144	33	2	17	88	.262	52	59	0	206	409	7	*.989
1996—Baltimore (A.L.)	SS-3B	*163	640	94	178	40	1	26	102	.278	59	78	1	233	483	14	.981
1997—Baltimore (A.L.)	3B-SS	•162	615	79	166	30	0	17	84	.270	56	73	1	100	313	22	.949
1998—Baltimore (A.L.)	3B	161	601	65	163	27	1	14	61	.271	51	68	0	101	265	8	*.979
1999—Baltimore (A.L.)	3B	86	332	51	113	27	0	18	57	.340	13	31	0	36	142	13	.932
2000—Baltimore (A.L.)	3B-DH	83	309	43	79	16	0	15	56	.256	23	37	0	56	134	5	.974
2001—Baltimore (A.L.)	3B-DH	128	477	43	114	16	0	14	68	.239	26	63	0	97	209	14	.956
Major League totals (21 years)		3001	11551	1647	3184	603	44	431	1695	.276	1129	1305	36	4192	8213	294	.977

DIVISION SERIES RECORD

RECORDS: Holds career record for highest batting average (20 or more at-bats)—.441.

| | | | | | | | — BATTING — | | | | | | | | — FIELDING — | | |
Year Team (League)	Pos.	G	AB	R	H	2B	3B	HR	RBI	Avg.	BB	SO	SB	PO	A	E	Avg.
1996—Baltimore (A.L.)	SS	4	18	2	8	3	0	0	2	.444	0	3	0	7	15	0	1.000
1997—Baltimore (A.L.)	3B	4	16	1	7	2	0	0	1	.438	2	2	0	4	4	0	1.000
Division series totals (2 years)		8	34	3	15	5	0	0	3	.441	2	5	0	11	19	0	1.000

CHAMPIONSHIP SERIES RECORD

| | | | | | | | — BATTING — | | | | | | | | — FIELDING — | | |
Year Team (League)	Pos.	G	AB	R	H	2B	3B	HR	RBI	Avg.	BB	SO	SB	PO	A	E	Avg.
1983—Baltimore (A.L.)	SS	4	15	5	6	2	0	0	1	.400	2	3	0	7	11	0	1.000
1996—Baltimore (A.L.)	SS	5	20	1	5	1	0	0	0	.250	1	4	0	4	14	1	.947
1997—Baltimore (A.L.)	3B	6	23	3	8	2	0	1	3	.348	4	6	0	1	14	0	1.000
Championship series totals (3 years)		15	58	9	19	5	0	1	4	.328	7	13	0	12	39	1	.981

WORLD SERIES RECORD

NOTES: Member of World Series championship team (1983).

| | | | | | | | — BATTING — | | | | | | | | — FIELDING — | | |
Year Team (League)	Pos.	G	AB	R	H	2B	3B	HR	RBI	Avg.	BB	SO	SB	PO	A	E	Avg.
1983—Baltimore (A.L.)	SS	5	18	2	3	0	0	0	1	.167	3	4	0	6	14	0	1.000

ALL-STAR GAME RECORD

RECORDS: Holds major league record for most consecutive games started—16. ... Shares single-game record for most at-bats (nine-inning game)—5 (July 12, 1994).

NOTES: Named Most Valuable Player (1991 and 2001).

| | | | | | | | — BATTING — | | | | | | | — FIELDING — | | |
YearTeam (League)	Pos.	AB	R	H	2B	3B	HR	RBI	Avg.	BB	SO	SB	PO	A	E	Avg.
1983—American	SS	0	0	0	0	0	0	0	...	1	0	0	1	0	0	1.000
1984—American	SS	3	0	0	0	0	0	0	.000	0	0	0	0	0	0	...
1985—American	SS	3	0	1	0	0	0	0	.333	0	0	0	2	1	0	1.000
1986—American	SS	4	0	0	0	0	0	0	.000	0	0	0	0	1	0	1.000
1987—American	SS	2	0	1	0	0	0	0	.500	0	0	0	5	5	0	1.000
1988—American	SS	3	0	0	0	0	0	0	.000	1	0	0	1	4	0	1.000
1989—American	SS	3	0	1	1	0	0	0	.333	0	0	0	0	0	0	...
1990—American	SS	2	0	0	0	0	0	0	.000	0	0	0	1	1	0	1.000
1991—American	SS	3	1	2	0	0	1	3	.667	0	0	0	2	1	0	1.000
1992—American	SS	3	0	1	0	0	0	0	.333	0	0	0	1	1	0	1.000
1993—American	SS	3	0	0	0	0	0	0	.000	0	1	0	1	2	0	1.000
1994—American	SS	5	0	1	0	0	0	0	.200	0	2	0	1	2	0	1.000
1995—American	SS	3	0	2	0	0	0	0	.667	0	0	0	2	1	0	1.000
1996—American	SS	3	0	0	0	0	0	0	.000	0	0	0	1	1	0	1.000
1997—American	3B	2	0	1	0	0	0	0	.500	0	0	0	0	4	0	1.000
1998—American	3B	4	1	1	1	0	0	2	.250	0	0	0	1	1	0	1.000
1999—American	3B	1	1	1	0	0	0	0	1.000	0	0	0	0	0	0	...
2000—American								Selected, did not play—injured.									
2001—American	3B-SS	2	1	1	0	0	1	1	.500	0	0	0	1	2	0	1.000
All-Star Game totals (18 games)		49	4	13	3	0	2	8	.265	2	3	0	15	27	0	1.000

500 CONSECUTIVE GAMES

Player	No.
1. **Cal Ripken Jr.**	**2,632**
2. Lou Gehrig	2,130
3. Everett Scott	1,307
4. Steve Garvey	1,207
5. Billy Williams	1,117
6. Joe Sewell	1,103
7. Stan Musial	895
8. Eddie Yost	829
9. Gus Suhr	822
10. Nellie Fox	798
11. Pete Rose*	745
12. Dale Murphy	740
13. Richie Ashburn	730
14. Ernie Banks	717
15. Pete Rose*	678
16. Earl Averill	673
17. Frank McCormick	652
18. Sandy Alomar Sr.	648
19. Eddie Brown	618
20. Roy McMillan	585
21. George Pinckney	577
22. Steve Brodie	574
23. Aaron Ward	565
24. Candy LaChance	540
25. Buck Freeman	535
26. Fred Luderus	533
27. Charlie Gehringer*	511
Clyde Milan	511
29. Vada Pinson	508
30. Joe Carter	507
31. Tony Cuccinello	504
32. Charlie Gehringer*	504
33. Omar Moreno	503

*Only players with two streaks of 500 or more games.

400 HOME RUNS

Player	No.
1. Hank Aaron	755
2. Babe Ruth	714
3. Willie Mays	660
4. Frank Robinson	586
5. Mark McGwire	583
6. Harmon Killebrew	573
7. Barry Bonds	567
8. Reggie Jackson	563
9. Mike Schmidt	548
10. Mickey Mantle	536
11. Jimmie Foxx	534
12. Willie McCovey	521
Ted Williams	521
14. Ernie Banks	512
Eddie Mathews	512
16. Mel Ott	511
17. Eddie Murray	504
18. Lou Gehrig	493
19. Stan Musial	475
Willie Stargell	475
21. Dave Winfield	465
22. Jose Canseco	462
23. Ken Griffey Jr.	460
24. Carl Yastrzemski	452
25. Sammy Sosa	450
26. Fred McGriff	448
27. Rafael Palmeiro	447
28. Dave Kingman	442
29. Andre Dawson	438
30. **Cal Ripken Jr.**	**431**
31. Billy Williams	426
32. Darrell Evans	414
33. Duke Snider	407

3,000 HITS

Player	No.
1. Pete Rose	4,256
2. Ty Cobb	4,191
3. Hank Aaron	3,771
4. Stan Musial	3,630
5. Tris Speaker	3,515
6. Honus Wagner	3,430
7. Carl Yastrzemski	3,419
8. Paul Molitor	3,319
9. Eddie Collins	3,309
10. Willie Mays	3,283
11. Eddie Murray	3,255
12. Nap Lajoie	3,252
13. **Cal Ripken Jr.**	**3,184**
14. George Brett	3,154
15. Paul Waner	3,152
16. Robin Yount	3,142
17. Tony Gwynn	3,141
18. Dave Winfield	3,110
19. Cap Anson	3,081
20. Rod Carew	3,053
21. Lou Brock	3,023
22. Wade Boggs	3,010
23. Al Kaline	3,007
24. Roberto Clemente	3,000
Rickey Henderson	3,000

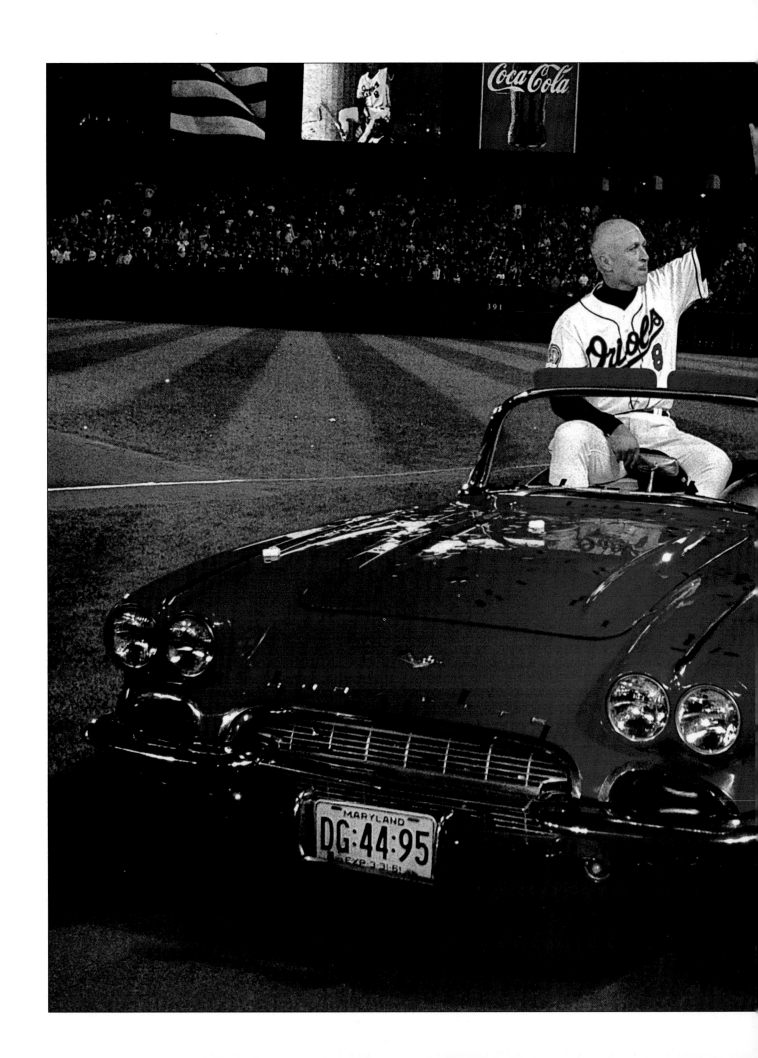